A self-taught chef's lifelong hunger, quest for knowledge, and desire for success—from struggling to survive in war-torn Italy to owning a successful restaurant in Houston, Texas

© 2019 Carlo Molinaro & John Dees

All Rights Reserved. No part of this publication may be reproduced, distributed, or transmitted in any form, including copying, recording, or other electronic or mechanical methods without expressed written permission of the authors, except in the case of brief quotations in reviews and other non-commercial uses as defined by copyright law.

Table of Contents

Introduction *Fine...e l'inzio*: Endings...and Beginnings   1

Chapter 1: *La Fame Comincia*: The Hunger Begins   5

Chapter 2: *Inspirzioni*: Inspirations   23

Chapter 3: *Un Cambiamento del Corso* A Change of Course   47

Chapter 4: *Parlano la Lingua* Speak the Language   65

Chapter 5: *Casa è Dove Si Rendono* Home is Where You Make it   87

Chapter 6: *Primo Piatto* First Dish   101

Chapter 7: *L'amore è Nell'aria* Love is in the Air   121

Chapter 8: *Modifiche* Changes   139

Chapter 9: *Arrivando in America* Coming to America   151

Chapter 10: *Citta di Asta* Boomtown   165

Chapter 11: *Il Sogno Realizzato* The Dream Realized   179

Chapter 12: *Lezioni Apprese* Lessons Learned   207

Ricette Preferite: Favorite Recipes   217

Fotografie: Photographs   235

This book is dedicated to my brothers and sisters, my daughter Sofia, my granddaughter Ella, Mary McBride Havard, and especially my sweet mama.

John would like to thank his wife Joy; children Casey, Caitlin, Courtney, and Justin; granddaughter Emma; and Butch & Julieann Hartman.

Introduction *Fine...e l'inzio*:
Endings...and Beginnings

Fame. Conoscenza. Successo. Translated from my native Italian into English: Hunger. Knowledge. Success. Three words. Three words that would drive me like a harsh taskmaster, inspire me like a muse, guide me like the great explorers from my native Italy as they navigated by the stars, leading me to my overall success in the challenging, yet satisfying, restaurant world.

I started life during World War II in Italy, always hungry—it was wartime and I was part of a big, poor family. I had a demanding father who took me out of school after second grade, forcing me to work at such an early age. I had a sweet, loving mama who inspired me with her words and encouragement.

I worked long and hard years as a busboy, waiter, maître d'hôtel, cook, and finally restaurant owner. I worked in restaurants and hotels around the world, including my homeland, Germany, Switzerland, England, Bermuda, and the United States.

After working for so many other people, I was driven to open my own restaurant. In 1982, I opened a small, twelve-table Italian restaurant in Houston, Texas, and called it La Trattoria. In Italy, a trattoria is a small, comfortable restaurant with satisfying meals at good prices.

My clientele including everyone from the rich and powerful, to the famous, to just everyday folks, all who loved my simple yet delicious meals. I even had a former President with a well-known dislike of broccoli tell me, "Chef, I don't know what you did, but I liked your broccoli." My little restaurant garnered praise from my customers, the press/media, and fine dining organizations, alike. The restaurant and my food won numerous awards.

I worked hard to build my business, striving to combine fresh ingredients into simple, classic Italian meals. I would drive for hours around the Houston area to buy seafood from the waterfront in Kemah, the freshest bread from a Mexican bakery, and seasonal greens and vegetables at the local markets.

I established long, personal relationships with my customers, greeting everyone as they came in no matter how busy I was. I trained my staff the way I trained myself, after learning in phenomenal high-end restaurants, hotels, and resorts around the world.

In December 2010, twenty-eight years after opening my dream restaurant, I decided to close. I was having health problems, and I decided to go out on top, on my terms. That's a long time for a restaurant, especially considering its location in the ultra-competitive dining and retail area of the Westheimer/Galleria section in Houston.

Overall, I had spent 50 years in the restaurant business. Not bad for a poor kid from Italy with no formal training who was forced to quit grade school.

I entered a restless, seemingly endless retirement. After the stress and frenzied pleasure of working with food and wine almost every day of my life, typical retiree amusements like golf, tennis, or bridge held little allure for me. I wanted to grapple with the lessons of my life. But I wasn't sure where to begin.

What I did know in some way—all I knew, in fact—was that the world and my profession had changed significantly around me. Chefs were now trained in a manner foreign to my often cruel, almost medieval European apprenticeship. They also tended to be different types of people, with wilder dreams and more opportunities to pursue those dreams than I ever dared entertain. The proliferation of cooking shows on TV, and practically every chef and celebrity releasing cookbooks, helped bring about these changes.

So today, many see cooking as a way to become famous. For me, Carlo Molinaro, from a tiny Italian village outside Romeo and Juliet's Verona, the single greatest attraction of the restaurant business was that it always kept you fed. During World War II and then in post-war Italy, that was attraction enough.

Initially, remembering the early period of my life, the only thing I could recall was being hungry. So I set out on a journey, searching for that different world, in many ways a lost one, which had taken this country boy from just outside one of Italy's most beautiful and historic cities and molded him into a battle-scarred professional.

After struggling with retirement, and seeing what the world of cooking had become, I decided two things: 1) I needed to tell my story, emphasizing that if I could start from nothing and run a successful restaurant for almost three decades, anyone could do it, and 2) I wanted to share some recipes that are special to me and reflect my homeland and experiences.

Also, I had to journey to the places where my winding path had taken me, both literally and figuratively. I would begin at the beginning, naturally, to seek out those stops on my long destination—to touch, feel, and experience them again. I hoped against hope that some of the people I had known were still around.

My journey, both to write this book and travel to my past, might feel like an Odyssey that Homer should describe, or maybe a large (and expensive) fool's errand. But I knew I had to do it. Life was calling me, not from my future as it had so long ago, but from my past. A past driven and inspired by those three words: *fame, conoscenza, successo.*

Chapter 1: *La Fame Comincia*

The Hunger Begins

Stomach growling...must eat. Many of my earliest memories are of being hungry. Hungry when I woke up and as I wandered the fields near my home in the Italian countryside. Hungry as I helped my mother prepare a sparse but delicious meal for our big, Catholic family. Hungry as I crawled into bed and fell asleep.

I was always hungry as a child, always trying to find something to eat, even if it meant getting in trouble for eating the neighbor's fruit or sneaking off during school to steal morsels from the local market.

It is understandable though, how hungry I always was. First, it was wartime. Most of the world was at war, but I only knew what I saw as a child in my village. Second, I was born into a large, poor family. There were ten of us, and I was the youngest boy. What can you say? We were Italian AND Catholic.

Still, the war and its austere aftermath were not the reasons for my continual hunger, and it wasn't necessarily my large family. The main reason I was constantly hungry is a painful memory—one that served, and still serves, to drive the constant hunger throughout my life. A literal hunger that morphed into a hunger for knowledge and success. That reason? My father, Santo Molinaro.

Why, you might ask, would my father be the reason for my hunger? He refused to do any form of work. He refused to get a job. He forced his wife and children to labor and then demanded every penny we earned, mainly to spend on himself. Yes, my father was a selfish man who insisted the man of the house eat most of our meager portions of food. Any food that was left got split between all the other family members. Slim pickings for the rest of us.

No, my father did not work hard from sunup to sundown, like other fathers in our village. Fathers that needed to sustain themselves to face the never-ending labors of the next day and support their families. My father? He did absolutely nothing.

Growing up, Santo never helped his family, either. He was one of fifteen kids—his family owning plenty of land and paying people to work them. But he never worked in the fields as his brother did, or anywhere else for that matter.

He was not like his parents or siblings, who were considered a respectable family. He was a *pecora nere della famiglia*—the black sheep of the family. *Non buono*. They say every family has one, and I know all too well that my father was definitely the one in his family. His own father always complained that he was good for nothing.

He had dark hair, a smooth tanned complexion, and was very suave. He was born in 1896, shortly before the arrival of the twentieth century. Although he was short, he lived life large. He was what we would call a playboy. My mama, Olga Bottegal, was five years younger than my father. She was born on September 14, 1901. She would live during a tumultuous and wondrous time in history, living through two world wars, the rise of automobiles, the invention of the airplane, and many other changes and advances. However, she would see and experience very little of this, in the tiny corner of the world where she lived.

To this day, I think of my mama as the most beautiful woman, *bella donna*, I've ever seen, although it is hard for me to conjure up how she looked physically. She was short like my father, which naturally explains me. She had shoulder-length blonde hair and light skin.

Not all Italians are dark and swarthy, especially those from the North. We lived in the Veneto region, the agricultural region that spread out to other parts of the Mediterranean, Europe, Africa, and beyond from the dazzling maritime empire of Venice. Thanks to the sea-faring Venetians, of which Marco Polo is the most famous example, there was a variety of contributors to the genetic makeup of Northern Italians. Thus, my family's gene pool included the influx of lighter skin and hair.

If I can barely remember my beloved mama, I've purposefully tried banishing my father to the farthest reaches of my memory for the way he treated his wife and kids. As I grew into maturity, I could at least understand a little about why my mama fell for him. He was a few inches taller than my mama, and he wore his black hair slicked in the style of the day. Although he wasn't tall, he was handsome.

I never saw him out in the world, only rarely around our home and in the village. I know he never held a single job, but I came to realize how his good looks and charm (to others, not his family) allowed him to make his way through life. When Olga met Santo, I'm sure he used his appeal and allure to woo her.

When they decided to marry, his own family begged her not to. "He will be no good for you or your children," they said. Their warning proved true, as events will show. However, she didn't listen. Her heart won over her head—she was Italian, after all. My sweet mama must have seen something in this self-serving, do-nothing man, something that captured her heart.

Shortly before their wedding, his family sold their land and divided the money among the members; it was a large sum for 1921: 1.5 million lire total (long before the unified European continent adopted the euro as the standard currency, Italy used the lire). At the time, Italy and the rest of Europe was gripped by a recession following the Great War, or World War I as it came to be known after World War II started.

The sum my father received was about thirty thousand U.S. dollars, but then it was a fortune. Times were definitely tough, but the Great Depression was still years away. Perhaps my mother thought the future looked bright at that point and their married life would start out right. It was not to be, though.

My father—despite all the newspaper headlines about the economic issues, the talk in all the cafes of money woes, the daily struggles to survive taking place before his eyes—decided to take a trip. He traveled to Côte d'Azur on the Mediterranean coast of France. This "French Riviera" was one of the first modern resort areas in the world, with seaside hotels, restaurants, clubs, and casinos. It became the playground of the rich, famous, and powerful. Nice, the largest city in the region, called like a siren to my father.

He took the entire sum of money given him and went on a gambling spree. *A fool and his money are soon parted.* That's what they say, no? Lady Luck did not favor him, and he lost all of it. Every last one of those beautiful lira gone. A sickening thought for people that work hard to make a living. Like me, as I labored for decades to earn money and try to save throughout my career.

The upcoming married life of Santo and Olga went from promise and security to uncertainty and poverty. I can't imagine what went through my mama's mind when that happened. She married him anyway, and they settled down in a small Italian town called Cerea.

Cerea is part of the province of Verona in the Po Valley of Northern Italy. People generally tend to associate Verona with one of the locations in Shakespeare's Romeo and Juliet or where those two gentlemen in his other play were from. But the region is also known as one of the most fertile areas in the country.

The region, home to the Po River, is also called Pianura Padana (or Padan Plain), and features many ancient, verdant valleys and a network of tributaries of the Po. It lies between the start of the Italian Alps running east to west, and at the end of the Apennines mountain range that runs north to south down the country.

The weather in the region is moderate, never getting too hot or too cold. Its proximity to the Alps, Appennines, and the Adriatic Sea in the east result in relative levels of humidity throughout the year. Summers are moderate and humid, while winters are mild. The subtropical climate and availability of water for irrigation mean the region is suitable for farming and ranching.

This region produces a majority of the agricultural products in Italy, including wheat, rice, corn, barley, sugar beets, a variety of fruit, and livestock. As the heartland of Italy's agricultural production, it has been vital to the economic, social, and political fortunes of the country since the Roman Empire.

Cerea was founded around the early tenth century as a *castrum*, or a fortification (a militarily defensible position). Prior to that, the area was part of the Roman Empire until the fifth century. Many of the villages and towns in our part of Italy, as well as around the country, looked very similar thanks to the Middle Ages' twin fascinations—commerce and defense. I would learn the importance of both in my long life, as events in my life would prove.

The village had a non-descript market square where merchants set up tables to sell their local wares, fruit, vegetables, and other foodstuffs. There was a main street and a handful of even smaller streets snaking off it. These, I now know after living in so many world capitals, were little more than alleys, where men, women, and children lived out their lives with little or no hope of ever living elsewhere.

When young couples got married, they most often moved in with whichever set of parents had a little room to take them, essentially a different alley from the one they grew up gazing on or maybe even the same one.

Our family home was a simple farmhouse that was reportedly built in the sixteenth century. If you've ever seen a movie set in a rural Italian village, you can picture what it looks like. The structure is a two-story, rectangular shape with evenly spaced windows and shutters. The walls are tannish-white stucco, the roof is made of red tile, and there is a stone courtyard in the front. In the courtyard area, there was a vegetable garden and an apple tree.

Only the first floor had electricity, part of a government effort spearheaded by Mussolini to bring electricity to rural areas. Our living area and kitchen were downstairs, while all the bedrooms were upstairs. There were still five of the eight Molinaro children at home. I shared a room with my older brother, while my sisters shared a room.

In this little corner of the Italian countryside, my mama and father settled and started a family. Thanks to the double dose of being Italian and Catholic, they had a big family: ten children. Only eight would survive beyond the age of three. There were five girls and three boys (one of the boys was me). Ines (nicknamed Gina) was the first born, in the summer of 1924. Severino, the first boy, arrived in 1927. Nerina, Severina, Mirella Clara, and Agostino followed, between 1929 and 1938.

I was the final boy born in the family, making my entrance in September 18, 1941. This was around two years after the outbreak of war in Europe. I joined the population of our little village of Cerea, around twenty-five hundred struggling residents at the time, just as the weather was changing from the typical warm and humid summer to the slightly cooler temperatures of fall.

Italy was ruled at the time of my birth by Benito Mussolini, who took power in 1922, two years before my oldest sister Gina was born. Mussolini led the country as a democracy until 1925, when he established himself as dictator. He called himself Il Duce or "The Leader."

Mussolini founded fascsism in Italy and formed a German-Italian alliance with Adolph Hitler. Italy, as part of the Axis powers with Germany and Japan, sought to recreate the Roman Empire by establishing dominance over the Mediterranean and by invading countries in North Africa and the Balkans.

So, I was born into a world at war. I was a late-in-life baby, and my mama had just celebrated her fortieth birthday a few days before I was born. She wasn't done with having children after me though. She would have one more child, a daughter Maria, three years later. One more mouth to feed.

At that time, there were four other children still living in our home, along with my mama. And sometimes my father. My mama was a saint. She had to raise us on her own, for most of the time. My father would disappear and stay gone for long periods. Where did he go? Who knows? But when he returned, he would demand tributes of food and money. He would then light up a huge, black cigar at night in the bedroom and proceed to fill the room with smoke. The cigar was worse than a smoking chimney.

Bless my mama. Most of my memories I have of my mama are her working. She was certainly the most caring person, working day and night to meet the many needs of her family and household. She was constantly cooking, washing, and doing all of the things women did in traditional societies with virtually no comforts or conveniences.

She was always working, working, and working, a lesson I observed and took to heart in ways I couldn't begin to understand at the time and at my age. However, she instilled in me a work ethic that I've followed to this day, and it was an integral part of all my success.

If she was not in the kitchen, she was outside washing clothes or tending to our little vegetable garden. I would help her in the kitchen, bringing her requested ingredients such as fresh peas or corn meal. Looking back, I can point to this as the start of my love for food and cooking.

Along with working hard at home, she also worked part-time on a nearby farm. She would do various tasks there and contribute her earnings to the family finances—or more like my father's pockets.

As a result, our diet was an occasional scrawny chicken when my mama thought it worth killing one, or maybe some basic seafood that had looked good to her in the market. For the rest of our meals, we ate the vegetables we grew in our garden that my mama tended.

Our regular meal, especially when the vegetables we grew were out of season, was the cornmeal known as polenta, often with a simple tomato sauce. Polenta was very, very inexpensive, so we had always had a big platter of it. Fortunately, we loved polenta. For breakfast, we had polenta and milk. For lunch, polenta and some sauce. For dinner? Polenta was more than likely what was served. My mama made our polenta-centered meals simply and deliciously. Simple, yet tasty. And perfect for a big family!

I was very thin though, as were my mama and my siblings—not surprisingly, and I remember no fat people around our village. There is no small amount of irony in the fact that our almost penniless family enjoyed a much healthier diet than most of the rich people I served during my decades in the restaurant business. Simple, fresh ingredients are key to a healthy diet.

Hungry as I was every day and night, I would scavenge the nearby orchards to feed myself fruit. In our courtyard, I would eat apples from our tree and vegetables from our garden. I especially loved our tomatoes. I'd sit outside in the sun and bite into them, devouring them. They were so red, sweet, and juicy that the liquid ran down my face and dripped onto my shirt. The apples were so crunchy, slightly sweet, with a note of sour. Fruit and vegetables in today's markets pale in comparison to what we and our neighbors grew.

Yet even with our apples and tomatoes, I was always hungry. Our neighbor on one side had a fig tree and a cherry tree. I used to sneak onto his land and jump as high as I could to pluck the figs and cherries from his trees. Our other neighbor kept pigs, and on top of his pigsty was a canopy covered in grapes. I used to climb over the fence and sit on top of the pigsty, eating his grapes.

One day I got caught. "Ahhh!" my neighbor shouted. "I'm going to get you this time. Come down, Carlo! I got you this time." I was so scared that I jumped over the fence and ran for my life. The neighbor never caught me. I don't know if he ever went to my parents to complain about their always-hungry son. He may well have. If the neighbor told my mama, she could have and should have scolded me or punished me, since she certainly didn't believe in stealing from other people. But as I recall, she never said a word to me about this. She must have understood. The neighbor certainly didn't tell my father, or else I would have been severely reprimanded.

She ultimately did find out about my food thievery, though. A sugar processing business was located nearby, and farmers would send their crop of beets there to extract the sugar. The beet-laden trucks would lumber through our town—the perfect opportunity to pilfer the sweet treat.

My friend Carlo and I (yes, sometimes there did seem to be a shortage of names in my life—long before I named my daughter after my wife, Sofia, when she was born in 1974) would chase the trucks and grab hold of the bed to pull ourselves up. We would select a few choice beets for our own consumption, then jump down and run off with the drivers being none the wiser.

One day, I mistimed my jump and whacked my chin on the truck. I fell to the ground, bleeding. A crowd of villagers gathered around, and someone went to get my mama. When she arrived, she tended to me. She also knew how I got injured, and why. She looked at me with a stern expression and said, "Carlo, I know what you were doing. You cannot steal anymore." I hung my head in shame. Disappointing her was one of the worst things I could do.

Being kids, Carlo and I would play games with rocks and sticks, since we didn't have any balls or toys, but we were most likely to forage for food together. Every day on our way to school, we passed in front of a convent. The convent was surrounded by a brick wall, and Carlo and I could smell the strawberries they grew from far away.

Once, we decided to scale the wall to take part in the tempting berries. The wall was very high for a small boy like me to climb over. On my second or the third attempt to scale it, I finally reached my hand onto the top of the wall. But a brick broke off and hit me on the head. I started bleeding and we ran away. I still have a little scar from that brick. I learned my lesson that day: don't try to steal strawberries from the convent. Maybe God truly is everywhere?

A small stream ran nearby our house. I would often go down there and play by it. Once, I noticed fish in the water. I wondered how I could catch them. Hunger finds a way and an idea came to me—I built a dam out of rocks and mud to create a pool where the fish would gather. The fish complied and swam right into the shallow pool, so I started to grab and toss them onto the ground away from the stream. My brother noticed what I was doing and came down to help. Soon, we had several good size fish to take home for dinner. I was proud of my effort, providing food for my family.

During school, I often snuck out to steal a piece of fruit from the market. I would crawl out through an open window in the bathroom and come back the same way. My escapades did get me into trouble. When the teachers caught me, they forced me to kneel in the corner on dry corn kernels. It was torture, theoretically enough to deter me from future escapes. But only theoretically. The most important lesson in my life to that point was learning was how to feed my constant hunger.

The few times my father came home, when he came home at all, he would eat much of the food. If there was ever a piece of meat on the platter, my father got that, as the man of the house. When my mama did cook chicken for lunch or supper, he would greedily eat most of it. We would maybe get a little piece to share among all of us. Occasionally, we would get our hands on a herring, but my father would eat that too. His wife and children could touch it and smell it, but he always ate it.

I remember that one time, my father brought a lot of sausages and meats into our house. A neighbor had slaughtered some hogs and needed a place to store the goods for a short time. My father had volunteered to keep it for him. I'm not sure why or how this arrangement was supposed to work—I was not privy to his affairs, obviously.

The sight of all those delicious sausages was so tempting to me. The aroma drifted through the house. I had never seen so many sausages at one time. Oh, how only one could satisfy my hunger for some time. My father noticed my interest, and threatened to severely beat me if I snuck even a small taste. The prospect of getting a beating trumped my hunger, so I left them alone.

He not only selfishly took much of our food for himself. He also took all the earnings that family members earned. My older siblings all worked and my father forced them to give him all the money they earned to him. My father didn't believe in working himself, but he was ever vigilant keeping track of everybody else's earnings.

He knew when each of his children got paid, and on every payday he showed up at his or her workplace to take away the full salary. Some of my sisters worked as live-in maids, and they were paid a small amount in addition to room and board. What little money they made, my father took from them. If he could have figured out a way to take advantage of their room and board, he surely would have.

My oldest sister worked in a pastry factory, and every Monday and Saturday my father would go there to get the money she earned. Finally her boss, having watched how hard my sister worked in the factory, decided he had enough. "Go away!" he shouted at my father. "I will not give the money to you. It belongs to your daughter. She's the one who works here—not you. Now get out of my place!" My father stormed off, furious.

My oldest brother worked in a furniture shop, and when he started to earn some money, my father bought a motorcycle. "That's for me," my brother told him. "I earned the money, so the motorcycle should be mine. I need it to get to work." "No," my father said. "This is for me. I bought this for myself."

My brother knew better than to argue. But he would get revenge. He dumped a cup of sugar into the gas tank when my father wasn't looking, then stood by to watch him take off on the bike. The bike ran for only about three- or four-hundred feet, and then stopped cold. My brother couldn't stop laughing and tried to hide it from my father.

My father took the bike to the mechanic and said, "There's something wrong with this. It does not run. Give me my money back." "Oh, *Signore* Molinaro," he said. "You are right. It is ruined. Somebody put sugar in the tank." "Sugar in the tank?" my father repeated, first puzzled, and then enraged.

When he came home, he roared, "Who put sugar in the gas tank? Who did this?" "I don't know," everybody responded, as innocently as we could muster. This was one of life's small pleasures we could all enjoy. We maintained a united front, and never revealed the identity of the perpetrator. My father never figured out for sure who had done this terrible thing to "his" prized motorcycle.

One day, one of my sisters decided enough was enough: she was going to earn some money for herself. During the day, she worked in a field harvesting rice, and gave all that money to my father. But secretly, she got a side job for a few hours at night and kept that money for herself. It wasn't long until my father found out. He beat her mercilessly. He forced her to give that money to him, as well.

My sister wasn't the only person my father beat. My mama, my poor mama, got the worst of it. He was always miserable and complaining. Whenever he had any kind of problem, he took it out on my mama. He beat her with his fists and kicked her. Powerless to do anything because of my age and small stature, I endured the screams coming from behind closed doors. I had no way to defend her from my father.

As a family, we did have a defense, and it was the only one we had. On many nights my mama grabbed my little sister and me, and we ran out to the barn to spend the night. We nestled into the hay and hid from my father. We spent many, many nights in the barn together. In the morning, we would sneak back in the house, and I would hear my father coughing. He coughed for hours. "When is Daddy going to die?" I asked my mama. "Oh, no He's never going to die," she said. "I will die before him. Your father is never going to die." The words of a true victim. He would outlive her by many years, and I believe her death resulted, at least indirectly, from his actions.

The Italian military began to falter in 1942, and raw materials and food were in short supply across the country. Mussolini was forced from power. Shortly after my second birthday in 1943, the new Italian government signed an armistice with the Allied forces, including the United States and Great Britain.

Hitler, not wanting the Allies to gain a foothold in Italy and threaten German-occupied territories in the region, launched a campaign to invade Italy. German soldiers even found their way to, and through, our small town as their forces flooded southward to fill in for the disorganized Italian army.

One thing my American friends today might not be able to imagine is what our experiences with the German soldiers were like. The soldiers were often in and around our village, some version of occupation I suppose. Seeing how hungry we all were, they often gave us food, sharing their own limited rations so we might go on living.

In front of our house, less than a quarter of a mile away, was the railway station. Behind our house, perhaps a mile away, was an ammunition depot for the Italian army (which became a joint Italian-American army base in the postwar years).

One day, planes crossed the clear blue skies and started dropping bombs on the railway station and the ammunition depot. Even at my age, I understood that the bombers might be American or British, flying missions from the green fields outside London or from southern Italy, which was in the hands of the Allies moving up from Sicily to take Rome.

Or the bombers might be German, knocking out train stations and ammunition to prevent them from falling into the hands of the Allies. We didn't know, and really didn't care. For us on the ground, the bombs were the same and could kill indiscriminately.

There was a bunker nearby our home. One day when the bombs began to fall, my mama shouted, "To the bunker!" She grabbed Maria, the baby in our family, her voice high-pitched and frantic. "Carlo, Nerina! Run!" We flew across the lawn, but Nerina tripped on something and gouged her leg. "Mama!" she cried in pain. What could my mama do? Her arms were already full and the bombs were falling. She grabbed Nerina by her hair and threw her into the bunker where our neighbors had already gathered. Nerina cried from her injury as the blood ran down her little leg.

We had to wait until the bombs stopped falling before we could tend to her wound. The German soldiers brought her medicine, cleaned her wound, and wrapped a bandage around her leg to prevent infection. I certainly can't say this made the Germans any nicer in general than history recorded. It's just a reminder that our interpretation of people is based entirely on how they treat us, seldom on how they treat other people.

Years later, when I went to Germany to work, I think my fondness and respect for German culture reflected my earliest encounters with soldiers who treated us so well.

Not everything that fell from the sky during the war caused pain and damage. Once, the airplanes on their bombing missions came under anti-aircraft fire from Italian forces. They managed to cripple a few planes. Days later, we discovered that one of the airmen had bailed out of his plane as it was shot down. There was a massive search for the airman, but he seemed to have vanished. The only trace of him was the enormous white parachute that had brought him back down to earth.

"Let's get that parachute," some of the townspeople suggested. There was a young woman in our village who was soon to be married, but she had no money for a wedding dress. A woman in the town took the material from the parachute, white silk, and made the bride-to-be the gown of her dreams.

By the end of the war in 1945 I was four years old. Mussolini had been caught and killed by a mob and Hitler committed suicide in a bunker in Berlin. The Axis powers surrendered. However, the misery and depravations brought on by the war did not end for the Molinaro family.

I was never entirely sure where postwar austerity ended and my father's heartless greed began. Food was still scarce. We still didn't have a lot of money. We never celebrated holidays or special occasions during the war, and after it there were still no celebrations: no birthdays, no Christmas, no Easter.

I turned five before my father gave me my first Christmas present: an orange. I wonder how he obtained it, considering that the stalls at the local market were severely limited in the goods they offered, due to the crippled distribution system left behind in Italy after the war.

Having never seen an orange, I thought it was a ball. Although I never had owned a ball, I had watched other kids in the village play with them on the street, fields, and squares. Naturally, I started to play with it. "It's not for playing," he shouted at me angrily. "It is for eating." I started eating the orange, just taking big hungry bites. But then he shouted that I had to peel it first.

Just one more of the hard life lessons I learned from my father. He never taught me anything useful, never talked to me about anything, never advised me or instructed me. My father had all the time in the world, but that self-centered man didn't care for me at all. The only time he bothered to talk to me was when he needed something.

Well actually, when I was five years old my father did teach me one thing. Of course, it served his interests. He gave me my first job. He taught me to beg.

Under the pretense of doing some kind of work at the local army base, my father took me with him. There was a lot of traffic at the guarded entrance. Many Italian and American soldiers were coming and going all the time. His big plan was to offer to cut the grass along the side of the road, while I begged for money from the soldiers.

"Carlo, you can sit here," he said, motioning me to sit on the ground. "Hang your head like this." He showed me how to drop my head to one shoulder and only look down. "Hold out your hand. And when they drop you something, say, 'Thank you for food.'" "Okay, Daddy," I said. "I'll do that."

So I sat there and begged money from the soldiers. That's what my father taught me to do. That was my first job. It was the kind of horrible experience that makes you determine you will never have to beg again. I've been through many tough times, and certainly through times in which my pockets were as empty as my belly; but I always worked, moving upward from one job to the next. And I never begged again.

But as horrible as that experience was, my mama countered by teaching me something that impacted me for the rest of my life: her belief in me and her support. One day, my mama and I were sitting on our patio in front of the house. We were probably shelling peas or some similar type of chore to prepare for dinner. My mama stopped was she doing and looked at me. "Carlo, I see great things for you. You're different. I know you will go far in this world." I looked back at her, soaking in the words.

I sat back under the apple tree in our courtyard, the one that my father would yell at me at for shaking to get an apple to fall. Those simple words resonating through me, even at my young age. I would take her words to heart and work hard. I wanted to prove her right and make something of myself. Something far removed from being a beggar, or living off the toil of others.

All the negatives in my life faded away. My mama expressing her faith in support in me cut through the hunger, the humbling experience of begging, the harsh ways of my father. Her brief words would inspire me and set me on a path like an explorer of old—they became my personal North Star to guide me over the course of my life and my career in the restaurant business. The future looked bright, but I was soon to find out calm waters do not make good sailors.

My special recipe for you: Polenta

Since this was a time in my life when we had very little to eat, we appreciated the simple things. In this case, my recipe is simple and straightforward: polenta. Polenta is inexpensive but versatile.

It can be dressed up in so many ways with different sauces and toppings; it doesn't soak up moisture the same way rice or pasta will. If you let it cool, you can slice it into pieces that can be grilled or fried.

When I make polenta, I'm transported back to the kitchen with my mama as she gathered the ingredients for our meal and brought a pot of water to a boil. I would stand near her, eagerly awaiting her request for assistance.

Here is my recipe, as my mama would make it. *Buon appetito!*

Serving size: 2

Ingredients:

4 cups water (option: use chicken broth)

1 cup corn meal

3 to 4 bay leaves

1 to 2 cloves

1 tablespoon butter

Salt and pepper

Directions:

1. Bring 4 cups of water to a boil in a 2- or 3-quart pan. Add the bay leaves and cloves to the water.
2. Slowly add the corn meal, quickly whisking it into the water.
3. Cook the polenta for 4 to 5 minutes, continuously stirring it until it is the consistency of a puree.
4. Add the butter, along with salt and pepper to taste.
5. Cook for one more minute and remove it from the heat.
6. Take out the bay leaves and cloves from the polenta, then serve the polenta immediately.

Chapter 2: *Inspirzioni*

Inspirations

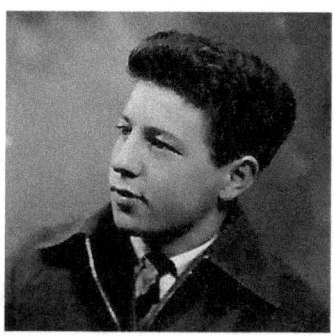

My journey beyond Cerea would not start just yet. However, I did discover the means that would start me on my path. Living in the country, our home was also close to another village, Sanguinetto. If you know a bit of Italian, Spanish, or even some French, you can guess that any village called Sanguinetto has something bloody in its deep, dark past.

Indeed, the village does. In the thirteenth century, it's said, an army from another town or city-state attacked the place. By the time the attackers were defeated, the moat ran red with blood of the enemy, and probably some defenders too.

The whole idea sounds preposterous to us now, as if Nashua, New Hampshire, attacked Burlington, Vermont. But that was Italy in those days, a place where loyalty to your town, your city, and your region mattered far more than any loyalty to some concept of a unified country. The people of the village looked down at the blood they had spilled, and the village was dubbed Sanguinetto.

Sanguinetto had little more to offer me or anybody else than Cerea did. Located about three miles apart, the two towns were my entire world. Sanguinetto did hold the rundown public school that my school-age siblings and I attended. Happily, there was one other feature of Sanguinetto, something that would prove quite important to my future. There was a train station.

No, we're not talking *Roma Termini* here, or *Santa Maria Novello* in Florence: these were big cities, important hubs of commerce and culture. Sanguinetto was just a starting point to journeys leading far away from the countryside.

Those big stations were about connections, made by buying a ticket or knowing the right people. People who traveled through those big train stations entered a sprawling, bustling, and always a little hectic, world.

Our little train station was silent a great amount of the time, and some of the trains that passed through didn't even bother to stop. We had just one *binario*, or track, where the people from our small world climbed aboard and disembarked, usually walking home from the station. If the traveler lived out in the country, like we did, they'd be met by a sputtering old car or truck. You might even see a traveler get a ride on a cart pulled by a very tired-looking donkey.

When I started school, I was six years old. Every day as I walked to school, I would look at that station and image what it would be like to climb aboard one of those trains and head anywhere. Anywhere but here. But that would mean leaving my mama and family. And I of course I was a little young to be leaving home.

I became vaguely aware that the station was the one thing capable of helping get me out of here. Eventually, it would. However, Cerea was my home for now. My place was with my family, and especially my mother.

I was very close to my mother and spent every day after school with her. When I was in the first and second grades, I would run home every day after school to help her in the kitchen or with work around our house. When she was cooking, she would say, "Carlo, go get me some tomatoes. Go get me some beans. Go get me some zucchini."

There was always something to do: we had five kids still living at home and many mouths to feed.

The second or third day of school, my mother had me follow her out the nearby street and gave me some practical advice that, as I grew to manhood, seemed to take on mythic proportions within my view of the world. "Son, when you walk on the street, you walk on the sidewalk, on the right side not on the left. Not on the streets. The streets are for cars, and when you cross the street you cross on the right-hand side. Remember that." A simple, but meaningful lesson. More than my father ever taught me.

She added, "When you see a policeman or a teacher, you greet them. Those are the most important people. The police keep you safe and the teacher educates you. Also, remember to have discipline and to respect others, just like you would want to be respected. Okay, son, don't forget these instructions. They will take you anywhere." *Disciplina. Rispetto.* Discipline and respect. These words would serve me well throughout my life and career.

I could not have had a better mentor in my life. My mother, as I believe a mother should, always made me feel special when I helped her around the house. It was never a duty, never a burden to do so. And it helped me understand the true nature of work. Through work, we express ourselves and use our God-given gifts while providing for the ones we love.

She had a vision for me. She told me she saw something in me that she didn't see in any of my brothers or sisters. "I see you will have a long career," she said one day, probably moments after I walked into her kitchen with my arms full of beans from the garden. "You want to go many places." I guess she sensed my desires to go and start on a new path, inspired my own personal gateway to the wide world: our local train station.

"Just remember, Carlo. Respect and discipline. That will always work for you. And whatever you do, Carlo, do your very best or don't do it at all. " I didn't completely fathom what she was talking about at the time, but later I would in turn live my life by those words.

Even though I didn't understand, I felt her special love for me. When she shared her vision for me, it was one of the first and only times I experienced such focused care and kindness. My older sisters and brothers were busy working every day, and although I think they also loved me, they usually had no time for me. I understand; they were wrapped up in their own lives. They kept their heads down and did what needed to be done to get through life.

Along with my mother's simple messages and lessons in life to me, I found a new passion at school. At the end of class, after some of the more official subjects a boy like me was expected to learn, my teacher would tell us about the adventures of our Italian explorers.

I loved to learn about these daring explorers. It was my favorite topic to hear about. Italy produced a lot of famous explorers, especially during the Golden Age of Discovery (mid fifteenth to sixteenth centuries). The names of those explorers still run through my head from those long-ago lessons: Marco Polo, Amerigo Vespucci, Giovanni da Verrazzano, Henri de Tonti, Giovanni Caboto and his son Sebastiano Caboto (John and Sebastian Cabot), and of course, Cristoforo Colombo (or Christopher Columbus, if you prefer).

Many of these explorers are well known, some less so. Marco Polo explored Asia, including China, and his writings inspired great curiosity among Italians and other Europeans. Amerigo Vespucci voyaged to the New World, and his first name is said to have inspired the word America. Giovanni da Verrazzano was the first European to sail into what is now the harbor of New York. Henri de Tonti traveled with the French explorer La Salle as they ventured down the Mississippi River and into the surrounding regions. Caboto and his son set foot on the North American continent before one of the most celebrated explorers, Colombo, navigated the Atlantic and visiting Caribbean islands in the "New World."

To me, these explorers were larger than life, and they inspired me. I dreamed of becoming an explorer myself, voyaging to distant lands like Asia where Marco Polo found his fortune, or having a grand vision like Cristoforo Colombo and setting my course to follow it.

I listened to the stories of these explorers that my teacher told, enrapt in every word. I was surprised when my teacher said, "Some of these people never went to school, but they had a vision."

No schooling, but still successful? Wow. That was a strange concept to me. I began to think about this. It seemed to me that the vision was the most important thing, not the schooling. This was an important lesson in life to me, the first I learned from someone other than my mother. Probably not the lesson my teacher wanted me to take away from the discussion, though!

I never thought that my own schooling would be cut short, but unfortunately, it would happen soon. I was blissfully ignorant of that future event looming at this point, and my priorities were helping my mother, finding food to eat, and attending school.

There were few games that I played in my childhood. What would I play? We didn't have a soccer ball. We had no toys. Nothing. I played by running around the front yard or around the little vegetable garden or charging up and down the nearby stream. On occasion, I would play hide and seek with my little sister. Oh, and my friends and I liked to play cowboys. Yes, even in a small village in Italy, we knew about cowboys and the Wild West. How? Our local Catholic Church showed Western movies for us. Odd, huh?

That was my first exposure to America. The land that many of those famous Italian explorers sought or even set foot on. I, like many other kids (and adults), thought America was a land populated by cowboys with six-shooters, good guys in white hats and bad guys in black ones, strong-willed women on the ranches and farms, and Indians riding palominos bareback.

America was perpetually stuck in the 1880s to us, a dusty and rocky desert landscape with wide open spaces, huge cattle ranches, one-street towns, and cactus everywhere. All thanks to Hollywood and its export of so many Western movies in the thirties and forties. I was mesmerized by these flicks. I just figured the American soldiers I saw after the war left their horses at home.

One day as I was playing down by the stream, I began to look for birds' nests. I loved birds. I loved to listen to them sing. And, in a way that only makes sense to small boys, I always tried to catch them. I approached a mulberry tree, looking up to see a blue jay sitting on her nest. I climbed up slowly, silently. Thrusting out my hand, I caught her! I squeezed her so suddenly and hard that she pooped on my hand. I couldn't wait to take the bird home and show my brother.

When I got home, I proudly showed him my prize. "How did you catch it, Carlo?" "I don't know," I said, "She was up in the nest, and I just caught her." We put her upstairs in a little cage and watched her for a while. I'm sure she wasn't happy about being rudely snatched from her home and thrown behind bars. As a young boy, I didn't think of that. I was about to learn another valuable lesson, this time from nature.

A few hours later we heard a tick, tick, tick on the window. I looked up and saw another blue jay tapping on the window. It was her mate, I figured, and he had come for her. My brother looked at me. "Carlo, you must let her go. She will die if she is not free." I knew it was the right thing to let her go. So we opened the cage door then the window. She immediately flew outside, joining the other jay in flight. As much as I wanted to possess that bird and keep her in my room, I had learned my lesson. No matter how strong your desire to hang on to something, squeeze tight and not let go, you must let go.

Although I would still wander the fields and play by the stream, I would not try to capture another bird after that experience. Speaking of the fields, my mother shared some deep spiritual advice with me related to the fields around us and nature in general.

My mother was a devout Catholic, by any measuring stick. She regularly attended Mass and took her children with her, making sure they went through Confirmation classes when old enough. Being Catholic, she gave birth to ten children, although a boy and a girl passed away as young children.

Once, we were walking along a country road as we came back from one of my Confirmation classes. She turned to me and said, "Son, if there is a God and He is everywhere, then you don't have to go to church. You can pray in a field, or anywhere." I'm not sure what motivated her to say this, and it was the only advice of a religious nature I recall her giving me. Sage advice from a deep religious thinker, yes? As a result, I actually do believe it's possible to pray to God in a field. Or anywhere, if you are so inclined.

As my second-grade year was finishing up, I started coughing. I couldn't stop. Day and night, I coughed. Time passed and I wasn't getting any better. Home remedies were not working. My strength drained and I got weaker and weaker. My mother was extremely worried.

We had no money to spare, but my mother would not let that deter her. She took me to the doctor. After examining me, he came to his diagnosis. "I'm sorry, Mrs. Molinaro," the doctor said. "Carlo has *la bronchite chronique*," he explained. Chronic bronchitis, an ongoing inflammation in my lung, resulting in a constriction of the airways. If not properly treated, it could mean a further restriction of the airways which causes shortness of breath, chest pain, and a strain on the heart. It can make a person vulnerable to other illnesses.

The doctor continued, "He cannot get better because he is too weak. And the truth is, he won't grow very much either. He needs more to eat. His breathing is very bad." "What can I do?" my mother asked.

"Feed him horse meat. He needs horse meat so his muscles can get stronger. Without that, he will only grow weaker." "Horse meat!" my mother shouted. "Horse meat! I tell you what, Dr. Altamura. You give me the money, and I will go buy my Carlo horse meat. How else can I get horse meat? We have no money, no money for anything."

We returned home, my mother determined to take care of me. She burned some eucalyptus root, wrapped it in cheesecloth, and placed it on my chest as a poultice. For a little while I would feel better. But soon enough, the coughing came back and I grew weaker. I began to worry that I might die. My mother was concerned, as well. Something different had to be done.

I finally became so frail that I was taken to a sanitarium, a hospital for boys with bronchitis. The sanitarium was located in Mezzane do Sotto at the foot of the

Alps, near Verona. This was a government-run hospital, meaning no one had to pay for treatment. This was a blessing to us, with our limited funds.

I was scared when my mother went to leave. I didn't want to be alone. She smiled. "Remember, Carlo," she said to me before she left. "Respect and discipline will get you through." She was positive and reinforced her message for me. She had faith I would pull through and continue on my path to a better life.

Along with her words, I would discover something inside me during this time: *persistenza.* I would need persistence to get me through my health issues. I would need persistence to get me through many challenges I would face during my life.

The hospital was full of boys, from toddlers to teenagers, all suffering from chronic bronchitis. The only remedy the doctors seemed to know was fresh, crisp alpine air and plenty of exercise. We ate breakfast, then went on a hike for two hours every day. Then, we would plod on weary legs back to the hospital for rest and relaxation. After that came lunch and more free time to rest. In the afternoon, we would go for a brief walk, followed by recuperation time and then dinner.

Although I was sick, I was grateful for the fact that I was regularly eating good food without having to scour the countryside to satisfy my hunger. One treat they gave us continues to stand out in my mind. Every day for lunch and dinner they gave us a warm, baked apple as a treat with our meal. I had never experienced such a delight before: food to fill my stomach and a warm apple to top it off. To this day, I love the flavor of baked apple.

Of course, the apples reminded me of home. I thought of my mother and family often and recalled her words to me. Even though I was dealing with a scary situation between my health issue and being alone in a strange place, I remembered to follow my mother's advice and treat the hospital staff with respect.

Thanks to regular healthy meals, coupled with the daily routine of exercise and mountain air, my fellow patients and I grew stronger. My cough started to get better; finally, it went away. I had convalesced in the hospital for nine months, without my mother and family. But I was well enough to leave. In July, I was able to return home.

I had lost almost a year of school and was looking forward to starting the third grade. "Daddy, when does school start?" I asked him excitedly. I knew I would start back to school soon, sometime in August. I just didn't know which date. I was so eager and anxious.

"Oh no, Carlo, you are not going to school," he said seriously. My look must have showed my cluelessness. What he could possibly be talking about? While I was away at the hospital, he must have realized that he needed to take advantage of my return. I was better, I had my strength back so why not put me to work earning money?

"I found a job for you in a bike shop," he said. "A job?" I asked. "I can't have a job. I need to go to school." I'm sure he sensed my growing desperation. "No, no, no," my father replied. "You went to the second grade. I only went to first grade, so that's enough school for you." I was devastated. How could he do this to me?

"You know how to count, right?" he continued. "Yes, but..." I stammered. "Then that's all you need," he snapped back. "There will be no more school, Carlo. You are only adding expense. From now on, you will work like the rest of the family."

That was the end of the discussion and the end of my formal school days. My mama was disappointed, but what could she do? Her little Carlo would have to get a job. Any education I was to receive from this point on in my life, I would have to make it happen. And my mama would also continue to teach me, in her own way.

My father's demand that I quit school and get a job started a fire in me. It was nothing intense a first, only the smoking embers that would later fuel a great desire in my life to learn, on my own, and succeed. Just as my mama's words had inspired me, my father's actions would motivate me as well. My father's negative impact in my life stoked my future path as much as my mama's positive one did. Two parents—one light and love, one dark and demanding—started me on my path. Colombo had his supporters and detractors. So did I.

The next day, as my father demanded, I started work. I woke up, and instead of walking to school, I walked the three kilometers to the bike shop where my father had gotten me a job. Instead of sitting at a desk in third grade, I walked into my new life as a kid with a job. Forced to work by my father, to make money for my father.

At the shop, my job had to be simple, of course. I was just a kid. I was tasked with testing the inner tubes to find any holes that would cause the bike tires to go flat. I filled the tubes with air then put them under water. I would then watch where the air bubbles came out. After identifying where the patches should go, the ties were repaired and refilled with air.

When I wasn't checking inner tubes, I was cleaning. Always cleaning, cleaning, and more cleaning. It proved to be good training for my later career in the restaurant business. Cleanliness in a restaurant was critical. Cleaning the bike repair shop let me use those skills to keep my workplace as spotless as possible.

I was around bicycles all the time at the shop. My mind would wander on occasion, as I thought of the freedom a bike could bring. How amazing it would be to zip around the streets of my hometown on my own bike. I really wanted one of my own but it was not to be. All the money I earned went to my father.

At the end of each week, my boss paid me six hundred lire. When I arrived home with my first week's earnings, I told my father how much I got paid. His response? He said it would be enough to buy milk for the whole week. For about a dollar a week, used to buy milk, he took me away from school forever.

I had worked at the bike shop for about six months, when my brother asked, "Carlo, why don't you come and work with me?" He had a good job in a furniture shop, making antique-style furniture. Furniture-making was the top industry of our region at that time. These furniture makers would disassemble older pieces of furniture, take the wood, and re-use it to make new pieces of furniture that looked antique.

"When are you going to work in the furniture business?" he asked. "Come with me." He swayed me to leave my job in the bike shop and switch to making antique furniture reproductions. After working for the business for a while, I decided I really liked making furniture.

It's a very precise process: repairing all the cuts and breaks and scrapes in an old piece of furniture, rebuilding pieces with different types of wood, then covering the whole piece with a one-eighth inch veneer of a fine wood, like mahogany. This is followed by endless sanding to make the wood smooth and perfect. After that, many coats of varnish are applied that will protect the piece.

I started to design and sketch things that I wanted to make, and I might have spent my entire working life making furniture. But my aspirations were distracted by a new interest. Our little railroad station and the nearby military base crept back into my thoughts. I noticed they required electricity, as did many of the modest homes around our village (as I said, one of the few worthwhile projects that came out of Mussolini's government).

I had always been curious about the power required to provide lights and run machines, when one day I realized, "Oh my God, so much is run by electricity." I was old enough now to pursue a new trade, a real trade, and I wanted to learn to be an electrician. I told my father what I was thinking. "No, Carlo," he said, again using his favorite word. "You would have to go to school to learn that. That costs money! You stay in the furniture business." Of course, anything that cost him money instead of making it for him would never happen. His selfish ways once again would squash any thoughts I had about returning to school.

So I stuck with furniture making, giving all my earnings to my father. Little by little, I started to rebuild my own pieces from start to finish, not just filling in a few details. I'll never forget my very first complete job, a Baroque-style credenza in two pieces. It took me almost a month to finish it. I was very, very proud.

I asked my boss to take a look at the credenza. He took one look at it, picked up a hammer, and smashed it to pieces. It was, he said, out of alignment by an inch and a half. "When you work for me, Carlo," he said, "everything will be perfect. I cannot sell this piece because it's crooked. It must be perfect."

I was stunned and dismayed. I went home that night and explained to my mama what had happened. "Oh, Carlo," she said. "He was right. Remember, I told you that you must do your very best all the time. You are learning, my son." That lesson, as hard as it was, stuck with me. From then on, whatever I did, I tried to do it perfectly.

My work in the furniture business turned out to be similar in many ways to the work I would do much later in restaurant kitchens—especially the care and precision required to make fine European pastries. In fact, I would use the same care and precision in all aspects of my restaurant career: planning, prepping, and preparing meals; cleaning; meeting with customers; working with other staff members, and so on.

I continued to work, walking there and back every day, no matter the weather or how tired I was. But, when I got a little older, my mother would surprise me with a wonderful gift. She knew how hard it was for me to get to work, as well as any other places I needed to go since I had to walk everywhere. I didn't know she had a secret plan (I presume my father didn't know anything about it either; he surely would not have approved). She'd been selling eggs and stashing the money away, hiding it from everyone. When she finally sold six hundred eggs, she took her money and bought me a yellow *biciclette*.

A bike! For me. After all that time I had spent working on other people's bikes, I finally had one of my one. It was one of the few possessions I would have as a child. I'm surprised my father didn't try to claim it for himself. But he let me keep it. I guess since I was riding it to work.

The bike meant so much to me, giving me a freedom I never had or knew. I was so proud of that bike. I even had a yellow jacket to match my bike. I looked sharp in my outfit as I rode my bike around our little village.

I went everywhere on that bike: to work, to the market, and just around town in the little free time I had. I would ride the streets and alleys of Cerea like I owned the place. The king of Cerea. Those alleyways I rode through were a world of their own. Everyone's windows all tended to be open along the alleyways, except in the coldest winter months, and it seemed like there were always someone in them watching the world go by.

Often, there were lines strung across the alleys, with laundry hung out them to dry. Women's slips, brassieres, and panties were across the alleys, offering me my first embarrassed glances at the world of women as I ventured around town.

I was starting to notice girls now, and my bike played an important part in my newfound interest. I paraded around in front of the girls on my bike, trying to strike up conversations with them. I would ride by the school and talk to the girls when they left for the day. One particular girl around my age would wave to me from her second-story window as I rode by. I would stop and sing to her. She would shyly smile as I serenaded her. Now I felt like another famous Italian, Casanova.

In my later years, I would always love the very best, and expensive, cars. I think I've sought in my later years to recapture those first feelings of freedom I experienced with my bike. Unfortunately, those cars seldom seemed to love me the way I loved them. Let's just say, I'm prone to accidents. I've been in several accidents and injured myself repeatedly.

That bike embodied the love and support my mama had for me. I treasured it. It would be one of the last, selfless acts she would be able to show me, though. The lives of the Molinaro family were about to take a tragic turn.

By the time I turned sixteen, I was a seasoned veteran of the workforce. I had put a few miles on the bike. This was about the time I started to notice some changes in my mother. She was always tired, and even complained about how tired she was, which she had never done in the past.

One day she asked me to go with her to see the doctor. We rode to her appointment together on my yellow bike, passing by the village cemetery. All superstitions aside, it was hard to ride past a cemetery without feeling a certain chill, an involuntary shiver.

"Son," my mother said as we passed the cemetery, "that's where I'm going when I come back." "Mama, what are you talking about?" I said, dread and fear in my voice. "I know you are so tired and exhausted. But you will be okay." In that moment, I believed my words to be true. I wanted them to be true with all my heart.

We arrived at the doctor's office, and she left me to wait while she went to be examined. After mama had only been with Doctor Altamura for a few minutes, he came out and grimly said, "Carlo, go home and tell your dad to come here right away." I felt a tightness grip my chest as my world started spinning.

I rushed home and told father that the doctor wanted to see him. My father left, going to meet with the doctor. The conversation did not take long. After their brief talk, my father immediately took my mother to make the ninety-plus-kilometer (about fifty-five-mile) trip by train to Padua, or *Padova* in Italian.

One of the oldest cities in Northern Italy, Padova is home to an *ospedale*, or hospital, at the Università di Padova. At the time, it was the largest healthcare facility in Italy.

That was at the beginning of the week. On Saturday, just five days later, I went to visit her, and I'll never forget what she looked like in that bed. She was yellow, just like a lemon. "Mama, how are you doing?" I asked my dear mama. "No good, no good. Son, listen to me. Take care of your sister Maria, because I'm not coming home."

"No, Mama, you will be fine," I said. "You'll be fine." I didn't want her to talk that way. She needed to come home to her family. Surely the medical staff could help her get well and back to us, like I was able to do. Her diagnosis was cancer, though, and she was in the late stages.

The following Saturday my brother came to the shop where I was working. "Let's go to Padova to see mother," he told me. "She is not feeling very well." I could tell from his tone that mama was really sick. We quickly packed a few things for our trip to Padova. Anxiously, we boarded the train from our little station, the one that would one day start me on my next phase of life. For now, it was taking me and my brother to see mama. It couldn't arrive fast enough for me.

The train arrived about two hours later. It was too late. By the time we arrived at the hospital, they were already putting my mama in a casket. She had passed away from throat cancer. She never smoked, but my father always smoked those huge black cigars in their bed. I always blamed that smoke, and indeed my father, for killing my mother.

My oldest brother and two sisters were already there at the hospital. I started to weep. My sweet mama was gone. She had once told me she would die before my father, and she did by many years. Her comment about the cemetery also ran through my head. She knew. At the time I had refused to accept her declaration: she would not return to her home, but to the cemetery.

There was a hole in my life now. The pain was so intense. I hurt, deeply. "Stop, stop, Carlo," my oldest sister pleaded as I continued to cry. "Leave him alone," my other sister said, taking my hand. "Let it out, Carlo. *Piangere*, my little brother, you cry. *Piangere*."

For three days and nights, I cried. I remember sitting on the train on the way back to our village with its tiny one-*binario* train station. My brother put his arms around me and said, "It's okay, Carlo. You're going to be okay." It would never be okay. I would never recover from losing my beloved mama. But he was trying to comfort me.

I think my siblings understood how close mama and I were. They didn't want to see me hurting like I was. They tried their best. When we arrived home, I just stared. A huge part of what made it a home was gone now.

I couldn't figure out how to be at home without my mama. My father, he was nobody. He wouldn't, or couldn't, take care of us. He couldn't cook or do anything around the house. Life had to go on, we just weren't sure how that was going to happen.

The next day, my mother's body arrived at our village church, with the funeral schedule the following day. It was an extremely simple service. Not many people attended, since it was a small village. We walked from the church to the cemetery, which was about a quarter mile away. I cried the whole time.

How would I survive now? What would I do now? My mama was everything to me.

"You will be fine," my oldest brother said, seeking to provide solace like he had on the train. Then he added, "Mama is in a better place." So many people around the world have used those words to provide comfort to others when a loved one passes. At that moment, they did not help me.

"But Mama isn't here. What are you talking about?" I shouted. In my mind, in her home with us was the best place. "She is in a better place," he repeated. "She is not here," I insisted, through my tears. "She's up there, Carlo. She's in a better place," he said. "Papà cannot beat her anymore." I stared at him. I begrudgingly admitted to myself that he was right. Father could not lay a hand on her ever again.

After my mother's burial, everybody just disappeared. There was no family gathering, absolutely nothing. I have no idea where my father went afterward, and my older brothers and sisters went back to their homes. I felt like everyone had deserted me.

Sometime later, my oldest brother, Severino, said, "You will come to Milano with me, Carlo. That's what you will do." Despite my pain, I considered his offer. There was little to keep me in Cerea now. Only my brother, Augustino, and my little sister, Maria, still lived at the house.

There was a lot of opportunity in Milano (or Milan), I now know in a way I couldn't recognize then. The fashion industry had taken hold there in the 1950s, and the economy was booming. For me, what was attractive was the number of furniture shops there.

Since I had experience working with furniture, Severino thought it would be best for me to move in with him and his wife. I could stay with them and pursue a career in furniture. "With the kind of profession you have, Carlo, you'll find a job immediately."

I had never been anywhere in my sixteen years beyond Cerea and Sanguinetto, other than to Padova to see my mama in the hospital and to nearby Verona a few times. Now, my brother was urging me to come to Milan. I wanted to go, but I didn't want to leave Maria behind.

Who is going to cook for her? I thought. I never saw my father in the kitchen or cook anything in his life. When my mother was in the hospital, Augustino prepared our dinner, but my father was not the type of person who would take care of anyone else. I was worried about my little sister. "I will send for you, Maria," I promised as I said goodbye. "As soon as I get settled, I will send for you." I never told my father that I was leaving.

Augustino took me to our little train station to buy my ticket to Verona. "When you get to Verona," he said, "buy a one-way ticket to Milan. Severino will be waiting for you in Milan." He seemed to think for a moment, then his face opened into a wistful smile. "See if you can find me a job there, too."

I boarded the train in Sanguinetto. I had stared at this station every day on my way to school, dreaming of where it could take me. This station had been the focal point of my desire for so many years to leave Cerea behind. To start down the path my mother had inspired, and tales of Italian explorers from my teacher had reinforced.

Now I knew where the train from the station would be taking me: Verona, so I could then take a train to Milan and my new life. It wasn't the way I thought I would start my journey into the wider world.

Once I reached Verona, I bought my ticket for Milan. I clutched my little bag that held the few clothes and small possessions I owned. Finding the line for Milan, I saw the train was waiting. The train was empty, I was the first one to board.

As I sat down, I noticed a brown bag on the floor, an attaché case. I looked at it a couple of times, not sure what to do, then grabbed it. I placed it on the seat next to me and pulled it open.

When I looked inside, my heart started racing. My mouth was suddenly parched. I was petrified. It was full of money—one hundred thousand lire or more. I had never seen that kind of money in my life. I'd hardly ever seen *any* amount of money before.

I couldn't think; I couldn't move. I was frozen stiff by this discovery. After a few minutes, I started to count it. I paused, then slammed the case shut and set it beside me for fear of being discovered.

What should I do? I wondered. *Maybe I should get off the train, take the money, and run away. Maybe I'll go down to the next station and take another train to Milan. With this money, I could be set for a long time. I could use it to help take care of Maria.*

I realized this money was a test. My mama's words leapt into my mind. *Don't steal, Carlo.* Before I could continue my journey, I had a hurdle to cross.

Right as I was thinking that, I heard a commotion. The noises were coming closer. It was the conductor and another man. They were looking left and right, peering into all the compartments.

When the conductor got to me, he pointed to the attaché case and said, "Is that yours?" "No, it's not mine," I blurted. They grabbed it and yanked it opened. When they saw that everything was intact, they were visibly relieved. They took the case and left.

The trip to Milan took about an hour and a half. I was consumed with thoughts about what had just happened. What had I just done? A couple of days later, I would think *how stupid I was. I should have taken the bag and walked away.*

But at the time, I had been petrified. I did not know what to do. In the end, in my indecision, I ended up doing the right thing in a way. The test was over. There would be no easy path to money for me. I would have to work for it.

As the train closed in on Milan, my thoughts turned to my new life. What kind of job might I get? What new things would I see? I realized I would be apart from most of my siblings. And of course, I would have to face all this without the most important person in my life: mama.

My journey was underway. As Colombo had set off to find the New World, I, in my own way, was going to a new world.

My special recipe for you: Pollo al Mattone

This recipe reminds me of home in so many ways. First, it involves chicken, which was the main type of protein we ate growing up. Second, this recipe dates back to one of the earliest civilizations in Italy.

Some Italian recipes go back to the Roman Empire and the legions who marched across the country, and on through other parts of the European, the Mediterranean, and North Africa.

When they passed through the region of Italy we know today as Tuscany, the Romans picked up this recipe from an even older civilization they had conquered: the Etruscans.

In English, this dish is often called Chicken Under a Brick. It definitely has many fans.

Serving size: 2

Ingredients:

2 14-ounce Cornish hens or small roasting chickens

2 lemons for juicing

1 cup extra-virgin olive oil

2 tablespoons paprika

1 tablespoon dried rosemary

Ground red pepper to taste

Salt and pepper to taste

Directions:
1. Split each chicken in half; cut down each side of the backbone and remove it. Cut through the breastbone from inside the chicken until you can fold it open like a book (leaving the skin in place).
2. Coat each chicken with olive oil and rub the outside with salt, pepper, paprika, rosemary, and red pepper.
3. Place the chickens in a refrigerator for 90 minutes.
4. Preheat the oven to 375 degrees; remove the chickens from the refrigerator.
5. Get a metal pot with a diameter less than your grill pan and fill it with water. This will act as your "brick." You can cover the pan bottom with foil for easier cleanup. Note: if you have two clay bricks available, you can wrap them tightly in foil and use them.
6. Heat a cast-iron grill pan on the stove to medium-high heat. Press one chicken into the grill pan, skin side down.

7. Place the water-filled pot on top of the chicken and grill the chicken for about 1 minute on each side. Grill the other chicken in the same manner.

8. Finish cooking both chickens in the oven for about 20 minutes until the juices run clear and the meat at the bone is no longer pink (a thermometer reading taken near the thigh should read 165 degrees F).

9. Plate the chickens, squeezing the lemon on top. Serve with roasted potatoes.

Chapter 3: *Un Cambiamento del Corso*

A Change of Course

When I got to Milan, I couldn't believe how beautiful it was. Even the train station was unbelievable. It was immense, and there were so many people, more people than I could imagine in one place. As I climbed off the train, I immediately saw Severino waving at me despite the crush of people.

We ran to each other, hugging and kissing the Italian way. "Let's go," he said, walking me out of the station. I stopped, looking all around. I was mesmerized by all the sights, sounds, and smells of Milan. The streets had so many people, flowers were blooming everywhere, and even the trees were full of blossoms. I couldn't stop looking around; I had never seen anything so beautiful.

Milan is located in Northern Italy and is the second largest city to Rome. It is the capital of the Lombardy province. It's only around two hundred kilometers (a little over 125 miles) from Cerea in almost a westerly direction, but it was a world away to me. It established itself as one of the leading European cities during the Renaissance and continues to be so to this day. For one, Milan is considered the world's fashion capital. The vibrant city is also known for its history, museums, arts, architecture, cuisine, and culture, drawing tourists from around the world. It is a leader in diverse areas such as furniture design, commerce and finance, healthcare, and education, as well.

Into this city—everything that little Cerea was not—I ventured wide-eyed and anxious. Despite feeling so overwhelmed by my new home, I was so happy to be there. My life in Cerea was behind me, as well as the pain of staying in the family home without my mother. That afternoon, a customer of my sister-in-law invited us to lunch. Following the introductions, we sat down to a wonderful lunch. I had never seen, or eaten, so much good food. I ate my fill, one of the few times I've ever had a full stomach. It was all I could do to stop eating.

I also experienced a wonderful wine for the first time. Even though I was still a teenager, it was okay for me to drink wine. This was Italy, after all. If adults thought you weren't old enough, you at least drank grape juice. The wine was called Fresa del Piemonte, and it was very soft, mellow, and slightly sweet. It would start me on my life-long appreciation of fine wines; I would eventually open a wine bar as part of my restaurant in Houston.

It was quite the celebration of my arrival in Milan. Even though my brother told me to stop drinking, I couldn't. I kept drinking until I started feeling a little drunk. It was my first time to feel that inebriated. Later that day, drinking that much caught up to me. I didn't feel well.

After that, I vowed to myself that I would never drink again! Of course, I would drink wine again, but never to the point of getting drunk. I certainly slept well through the night after that amazing lunch, with a sated appetite and alcohol coursing through my body.

Severino had lined up a job for me, but it was making modern furniture, not antiques like I had been trained to work with. Why would he set me up in a modern furniture shop when I was trained in antiques, I wondered? They are a different as Michelangelo and Picasso.

Modern furniture is totally different. You work on a machine, not with your hands. There is no carving or shaping of the wood. You simply cut the wood, glue it together, sand it down, and polish it.

But a job was a job. I would walk to work six days a week, once again. I left my beloved yellow bike back in Cerea. At work, we would make several pieces in one day in assembly-line fashion. I would glue the cut pieces together. I would then pass the assembled pieces to the next person for sanding, who would pass it to the next person for polishing.

It was a very simple work, my first time on an assembly line. There was nothing artistic about it, like with the tasks I performed at my previous furniture job. I didn't mind though, because I had escaped my small town and was now living in such a beautiful, bustling, big city.

Later, in my career in the restaurant business, I came to despise the assembly-line approach that many dining establishments would embrace. Not just in the kitchen, but in the dining area. The whole point is to get people in, feed them quickly, take their money, and get them out so more people could be served. It's one thing to efficiently prep for a meal, but another to rush guests in and out. I approached guests differently in my restaurant; I would offer dining parties that were finishing up a drink at the bar. It would free up the table for the next party, without making anyone feel rushed.

Life with Severino and his wife was good. We all worked and came home around at six in the evening, then my sister-in-law would prepare us a meal. I was happy to have food. It wasn't much, and I was still always hungry. However, I didn't have to scrounge around orchards or steal grapes from atop a neighbor's pigsty. So, it was a step up from those lean times in Cerea.

I was grateful that my brother had convinced me to come to Milan. If I had stayed in my own little town, I don't know what kind of life or future I would have had. Italy had mandatory military service requirements for males aged eighteen and over. I probably would have served my time in the armed service and my life would have taken a different turn. Because I was working though, I was able to apply for an exemption.

Speaking of Cerea, little Maria was still at home. She wrote me several times, asked if I could find her a job. "What kind of job?" I wrote back. "You're only fourteen years old." Of course, I wasn't much older, but I had worked for several years now. "I can work as a maid or in a grocery store," was her reply. I could sense her desperation.

I thought long and hard about how I could get my baby sister a job and away from my father. Plus, when my mama was sick, she had asked me to take of Maria. I had to find a way. Somehow, I got connected with the owners of a grocery store that was not too far away from my new home in Milan.

I went in one day and asked if they had any jobs available. "Oh, yes, we are going to need some help here," they told me. I was elated! I could help Maria get a job and come join the Molinaro family whose presence in Milan was growing.

I wrote Maria a letter to tell her the news. As quickly as she could manage, Maria packed her meager possessions and boarded the same train I had to Verona and then Milan.

Next thing I knew, she was working at the grocery store and staying with one of our older sisters who was already living close to Milan. I was relieved that she had escaped my father's household for good. I was so happy for her. I knew mama would be happy, too.

After I'd been in Milan for about five or six months, I started getting very bored with my work. I told one of my colleagues, "I was not trained for this. I worked with antique furniture for the past three years. There is nothing to this modern stuff."

My co-worker thought, for a moment, then gave me an answer that thrilled me. "Carlo, I think you should work down the street," he said. "There is a store that repairs antique furniture." *What? that's fantastic,* I thought. "Will you take me there?" I eagerly asked him. So, he took me there and I introduced myself to the owner. Luckily for me, the company indeed had a need for my skills.

A week later, I started my job there. The work wasn't hard, but it was far more interesting than what I'd been doing. The owner was very happy to have me, my skills, and my work ethic. I was very happy too, because I was surrounded by the type of furniture I loved. Antique is my preference over modern. People would bring in their chairs or tables in need of repair, and I would fix the piece. Maybe a leg was broken or the surface was scratched. No matter, I could take care of it.

For me, these were very easy tasks since I was fully trained to build the furniture; to fix it was so much easier to me. Sometimes, I would leave the shop and travel to the customer's home so I could fix the furniture there. If it was a big piece that wasn't easy to move, I would go there and fix it right away. The customer always appreciated my work, since I continued to heed the advice of my mama to always do my best.

A few months after starting in my new position, I went out with some friends one night to play table soccer (or foosball). As we played game after game, I heard this one guy in our group happily talking about where he worked as a bartender. My ears perked up when I heard him say, "They give me lunch and dinner there." "Roberto, what are you talking about?" I asked, feeling my stomach growl at the mention of food.

"If you work in a restaurant, you get fed," he said. "Wow," I responded, the gears starting to turn in my head. "It must be delicious," I added. "Yes," he said. "It is very good." This captured my interest. A way to satisfy the hunger I've felt all my life, and get paid for it? Yes, please.

About a week later I saw Roberto again. I'd been thinking about what he said the entire time. If I could get paid AND fed, that would be the greatest job for me. I just came right out and asked him. "You know what?" I said, "Why don't you find me a job?" "The Caffé Grande Italia," he said. "They are looking for help." "Take me there," I said matter-of-factly.

At the time, I was only vaguely aware of how this simple discussion could forever change my life. Looking back, I recall how I believed furniture making and repair to be my career for many years to come. I see now I was poised on the edge of a defining moment. My life was about to change course.

A few days later, Roberto took me to the restaurant. The maître d' interviewed me for a busboy position. I didn't want to fail the interview, to not make a good impression, so I pulled out a small notebook and took notes. I was hired on the spot, despite not having any prior experience in a restaurant. Sure, I was only a busboy, but I had my foot (and stomach) in the door.

I had only *been* in a restaurant two or maybe three times in my life; the ones I had been to were not much more than a home kitchen with a few tables. Cerea and Sanguinetto were not known for their fine dining. Or any dining. And of course, eating out at a restaurant cost money, which we didn't have.

The minute I walked through those doors, I knew I had found my profession. It was love at first sight. I was enchanted by every part of it. This place—it was magnificent! I had never seen a place like this, except in a movie. I felt so attracted to it. I'm not sure why; I guess I just connected to it on some deep level.

The restaurant was not only a place of beauty, but it solved another problem: I would not go hungry again. I would not only get paid, I would get dinner. This was the ultimate job for me. No more working with antique furniture. I was hooked on being in the restaurant business.

I could not believe the luxury and the ambiance of the place. The whole system I sensed had been hammered into place and refined to make food preparation and service an efficient, gracefully designed machine. It was so gorgeous, and in some ways like the best furniture I'd made and now repaired: classic and beautiful. I admired this restaurant, and the more I saw and thought about it, the more I marveled.

The restaurant looked a bit like La Scala, the famous, international landmark Milan opera house that was just around the corner. The affluent people of Milan would attend opera performances dressed up in their fancy clothes. Our staff all dressed like those rich people, or at least our version anyway. The maître d' wore a tuxedo. All the waiters wore dark pants, a dark tie with a white shirt, and a white jacket.

Even the busboys dressed elegantly. As a busboy, the uniform they gave me included a short jacket with a bright bow tie. They gave me two uniforms, so after two or three days of using one I could drop it off at the cleaners.

As I was still settling into the restaurant's routine, I kept up my habit of writing everything that the maître d' told me to do in my notebook—exactly how he told me to do it. When I went to work every day, I would pull my notebook out of my pocket and read over the notes. I would study them just like I was in school. I worked hard to commit everything to memory that I was taught. You must make a commitment to do your best, and when you work hard, you can start to be a restaurant professional.

Every day at the Grande Italia was an adventure. To me, it was like living in a movie. I got to see lots of powerful and famous people in the restaurant. I particularly remember one person, from America. The maître d' called all of us after lunch and told us this American came to the restaurant every year. He said we had better take extremely good care of this man.

The very next day, the American came in with a box of cigars. The maître d' gave each of us a cigar from the box with the man's compliments, as he always enjoyed both the food and service. I don't recall if I wondered about where his six guns were, though. Could it be not every American strapped on belts and holstered pistols, ready for a gunfight?

When my shift was over, I went to the employee dressing room. The first thing I did was light up the cigar. Within a few minutes, I started to get dizzy and then I threw up. This was my first time to smoke—and also my last. Which is just as well, considering I still blamed my father's cigar smoking as the cause of my mother's fatal throat cancer.

While I was working at the Caffé Grande Italia, I would walk past another restaurant every day, called the Biffi. I was mesmerized to see its waiters in their black tuxedos and bowties, starched white shirts, and white gloves on their hands. I had never seen a waiter wear white gloves before, and I caught myself wondering how they kept them clean when they worked with food all day long. I imagined myself wearing gloves while working at my current job, and tried to picture how to clear dirty plates, cups, and glasses throughout my shift without soiling the gloves.

The Biffi was a city landmark, open for over a hundred years. It is located in Galleria Vittorio Emanuele II, one of the world's oldest shopping malls. The mall dated back to the mid-nineteenth century and was named after the first king of a unified Italy. Few cities are as famous for shopping as Milan.

The Biffi stands at the steps of the Duomo, the cathedral that is one of Milan's most famous landmarks. The restaurant's tables spill out its doors onto the piazza. It is a popular, elegant place to dine. I told myself that one day I will work there.

The Galleria connects the Piazza del Duomo to the Piazza della Scala under a glass canopy, a type of soaring arch. I would stroll through the Galleria, gazing inside each restaurant I passed, wondering what it would be like to work there. Another restaurant, open for as long as the Biffi and just as famous, was the Savini. I could work at either place, I decided. My mama had told me I would go far, and either of those restaurants was a big step up from the Caffé Grande Italia.

Looking back, I think it's interesting that my first restaurant experience was in Milan with its Galleria, home to shopping and fine dining, while my restaurant in Houston was located near a glittering retail complex also called the Galleria. Sometimes life can symbolically come full circle.

I was not ready yet to apply at either the Biffi or Savini. I continued to work, learning as much as I could. After seven months there, I felt I was ready. I put on my nicest clothes, took a deep breath, and set forth to the Biffi.

You will never go anyplace, I reminded myself, if you are not willing to be adventurous and turn a new corner. Oddly, I was not the least bit afraid they might tell me I wasn't ready. If I was turned down, I would keep learning, do what I had to do to improve, and apply again later.

So, I confidently went to speak with the manager. He dismissed me almost immediately! I barely had a chance to speak with him. I was perplexed and astonished at the reason he turned me down. "You are too short," the manager said. "All of our wait staff must be at least five feet eight inches tall."

I was too short? I could not believe it. The Biffi's waiters and busboys were hired because of something they had no control over? I was five-foot-two, maybe five-foot-three if I drew myself upright enough. This height issue was not something I could correct. I could not go away, grow another six inches, and come back next week and reapply.

I was astonished at this requirement, since it had never been an issue with me before. This was my first setback in my budding restaurant career. I wanted to move up and felt I was ready. But the Biffi had a policy, they wanted their staff to look the same not only in their dress but also in their stature.

The realization struck me. I would never work here. No matter what I did, no matter how hard I tried, no matter how skilled I became, I would never be hired at the Biffi. I felt the sting. I had to deal with it and move on.

Many years later in another country, my adopted home of the United States, I would see the benefit of having books full of laws prohibiting such discriminatory hiring practices. However, Italy did not have such laws. I had to swallow the bitter pill and move on.

So, I went back to the Caffé Grande Italia feeling rejected and dejected. Despite my disappointment, I reassured myself I already had a pretty good track record for getting hired. And I had no intention of being a busboy the rest of my life.

I wanted to move up in the restaurant industry. To do that, I had to go from place to place to get lots of different experience, to learn new skills and work with a variety of systems. I was not primarily focused on earning more money.

I understood why money was not my primary motivation at this point. I saw that the real wealth lay in knowledge, in education. I sought to learn all that I could, soak it in. I had, after all, been robbed by my father of a basic education. Once I gained the required skills, I figured the money would come.

Also, I was a man of simple needs. By not having my own money for so long, I really didn't know what to do with it once I got it. I was living with my brother and his wife, I didn't need or have a car, I had no need for expensive clothes, I had no steady girlfriend, and I certainly wasn't going to waste money on boozing and carousing.

Anyway, I was not going to let anyone else out in the working world rob me of the opportunity to learn, to better myself, to advance. Including the Biffi. I also realized I would never learn all that I needed to at my current job. Surely, I told myself, most restaurants would not turn away hardworking staff because they were a few inches too short. I know what my mama would say. *Carlo, don't settle. Continue on your journey.*

With that in mind, I thanked the Biffi manager, walked out the door and across the street to the Savini, and applied for a busboy position. They immediately hired me—no height requirement there. I would take my next step on my journey upward.

The Savini was an impressive restaurant, with an equally impressive clientele. Located close to the famous Manzoni theatre, it boasted many high-profile customers, including such movie stars as Charlie Chaplin, Frank Sinatra, Ava Gardner, Lana Turner, and even Grace Kelly and her new husband, Prince Rainier II of Monaco. During my time at the Savini, I saw Italian movie stars Gina Lollobrigida and Sophia Loren with her movie producer husband, Carlo Ponti. They were big stars in Italy and they successfully got into movies made in Hollywood.

I didn't go to the movies much in Milan; I didn't need to. My life was like a movie and I had famous people around me all the time. Imagine me, a boy from a small town in the country, working in such a place. My mama would have been amazed and proud.

The restaurant also attracted countless Italian politicians eager to see and be seen. Most of the politicians who came in I had never heard of before. I wasn't much interested, really. Staff would say, in hushed tones, "See that man? He is the chairman of the Democratic Party." They were all impressed. But it meant very little to me. I would nod, but all I was interested in was learning as much as I could about the restaurant business.

Spotting famous faces dining in the restaurant would do nothing for my career, I felt. Thoughts of food preparation and service occupied nearly all my waking moments. I was obsessed with learning more. My education was continuing, starting the slow but steady advance from the dining room to the kitchen. I longed to go behind the swinging doors and work there, where so much of the magic that is a good restaurant actually happens.

Every time I entered the kitchen at the Savini, I would study the cooks. I would watch their efficient movements, how they prepared the various dishes, and the dishes' presentation. I also thought, as I watched them speed through their paces, of my sister-in-law's cooking at home. I realized the difference between the home cooks I had experience in my life and restaurant chefs was significant.

As good as Severino's wife's food was, what surrounded me now at the Savini could never be thought of as the same thing. They were worlds apart, like modern vs. antique furniture. This was art. Simple, fresh ingredients blended together likes the notes in a Beethoven sonata.

I briefly considered going to culinary school and becoming a chef, but that would cost a lot of money. Money I simply didn't have now. I thought about how I could gain such skills, without having to spend any money. I came upon an idea. I knew how I could benefit without going to a formal school. I would attend the school of life: I befriended the chef.

What better way to learn? Instead of spending money and taking time out to go to a formal school, where I would be one of many students, I would get some one-on-one lessons. What I would try would cost a lot less and benefit me more. It would only cost me some wine.

"Hey, Chef," I'd say, "Look! Table number twelve left some wine. Why don't you take it?" He would give me a quick smile and a thank you for the open bottle I'd brought him. At the very least, he could use such wine in cooking his next dish. More than likely, though, he would sip it after he finished his shift or maybe on a break during the long evening.

After employing this tactic for a while, it was time for step two of my plan. I summoned up the nerve to ask the chef questions about food and what he does. At first, he brushed me off. A kitchen can be a hectic place, not conducive to chit chat. I persisted though, and the chef relented.

"Okay," he said, a little worn down from all my questions about this fish or that sauce. "When you are not so busy, I'll show you how to do it." I kept my trusty notebook and a pencil in my pocket. Every chance I got, I'd copy down recipes and try to make the dishes at home for Severino and my sister-in-law.

The first few times, my attempts to make the recipes were a disaster. (Okay, so it was more than a few times.) But, with practice—lots and lots of practice—my cooking started in improve.

One dish the chef taught me to make was the city's famous local signature dish, risotto Milanese. It was simple: risotto with saffron. I went home and tried my hand at making it. After sautéing the rice, I added some broth and then the yellow-orange strands of saffron. But the saffron, one of the most expensive spices, didn't dissolve properly. To my dismay, the rice didn't turn its signature rich golden hue. I went back and explained to the chef what happened. "When is the time to add the saffron?" I asked.

"You put it in the chicken broth," he said, "not the rice." He continued. "When the chicken broth simmers, you dissolve the saffron in the broth, and then you add the chicken broth to the rice, bit by bit, not all at once, and cook it slowly."

He explained you only add more broth to the rice when it gets thick enough that you can see the bottom of the pot when you draw the spoon across. "And then you stir. And you keep stirring." A great tip. That's the type of information that a chef knows. Like pearls of wisdom from a learned *professore*.

I would go home each night and practice. If I did something wrong, I would recount to him what I had done the next day. He would say, "No, no, you've got to do it this way, this way, *this* way." So, this is how I learned. Who needed to pay for culinary lessons when I was getting one-on-one instruction?

On my way home from work I would pass through Piazza Missori. Located there was a very beautiful hotel called Hotel Cavalieri. Out of curiosity one day, I went in the employee entrance to ask if they were hiring. Someone told me yes, they were. The next day, I brought my resume and applied for a position as a waiter.

It was just a spontaneous act on my part. I think this was because I kept wanting to learn new things, experience new situations in the restaurant business. I was hired and started working there a few days later. I finally had transitioned from busboy to waiter!

The restaurant was on the tenth floor of the hotel, with a beautiful terrace overlooking downtown Milan. We served a lot of customers on that terrace. We used a very traditional service style. All the food would come out from the kitchen on a silver tray, then the captain and I would transfer the food from the silver plate to the regular customer plate. We would serve this way to each person at the table, always from the left side of the guest (you pick up the plates from the right when they are done). The job was, and had to be, very precise and organized between the kitchen and the servers.

I learned a lot of new things at this job. The manager would run regular meetings every other month; attendance was required. All waiters were expected to listen and learn during these meetings or else they would be fired. These meetings helped me learn so much about working as a waiter in a restaurant.

I worked at the Cavalieri for six months, until one day I was told by a colleague that the best seafood restaurant in Italy, called Aldo, was around the corner. My restlessness and desire to continue learning more had built up. I applied for a waiter position at Aldo and got the job.

I had never seen a restaurant like Aldo. The place specialized in seafood and they had a wide variety of shellfish and finfish that I'd never seen or even heard of at any other restaurant. Other places had some seafood, of course, but this place seemed to have everything that knew how to swim. The restaurant featured a rotunda in the middle, full of seafood. Some of it was still alive. Later, I would see this same approach in the Food Court of Harrod's in London.

My plan to bring wine to the chef had worked so well at the Savini, I decided to try it again on Guido, the chef at Aldo. It worked and we soon became friends. He taught me some excellent recipes, while he got to sip on some marvelous wines that neither of us would have been able to afford in our lives outside Aldo.

Guido also taught me specifics about many seafood types I'd barely heard of—expensive items like lobster, tuna, flounder, and Dover sole (remember, I was from a little land-locked town in Italy). Learning more about seafood expanded my recipes beyond my current skill set.

I knew then that I was hooked, pardon the pun. I realized I was fascinated by the art and science of cooking. Yes, I started to see that cooking is both an art and a science. Some dishes, like pastries and baked goods, require precise measurements and temperatures to work. Other dishes, like sauces, were more of an art, as the chef seasoned them to taste.

Little by little, I was transitioning from my role in the front of the house to the back, although any real opportunity was a ways off. I still had much to learn. In hindsight, I know that working both sides of the house helped me be so successful at running my own restaurant. In some restaurants, the waitstaff and kitchen staff do not get along. It's like a rivalry. I did not want that to happen in my restaurant, and it did not: the two sides got along well, because I encourage that good working relationship and set the example.

One other memory of Aldo makes me smile. The boss kept a green parrot perched on a stand by his desk, and each time a guest would enter the restaurant, the parrot would fly like mad over to the entrance and start chirping *buon giorno*. Whenever guests left, the parrot did the same, this time bidding them *arrividerci.* It was so unique. When I was planning my restaurant, I considered trying to find and train a bird to do the same. I scrapped this plan.

I would hang around with the other waiters, and our conversations would always turn to jobs: mainly, where to go to work next. We shared all the facts and fictions we heard from friends at other restaurants, about this place being great or that manager being a monster. We talked about how, or even if, we might fit in at those other restaurants.

One of the themes of our conversations was that if you spoke more than just Italian, you had a far greater chance of getting hired by the better restaurants. You could perhaps become a manager yourself.

This planted the seed of an idea in my head. I only knew Italian, and a few other words in some other languages. What if I could learn another language? If I could learn German, or French, or English, that could help my career greatly.

It would require discipline, and I could relate to discipline. My mama often told me that discipline, and respect, were key. Isn't speaking to someone in their own language, which is different from yours, respectful in a way? My mama's advice would never fail me.

In America, we think there's a sense of pride in being a professional waiter in Europe. Which is true. But that didn't mean, with all respect for waiters everywhere in the world, that we wanted to be waiters all our lives.

We want to move to a higher position, one that will pay better and let us use the new knowledge we gathered under difficult conditions every single day to better ourselves.

I decided not only did I want to learn more now, I was also ready to make more money. This drove me to visit an employment agency. My life was about to change course once again, this time taking me outside of Italy.

My special recipe for you: Seafood Salad

Seafood salads are always a hit, especially for those seeking something light, healthy, and delicious at meal time. I learned this basic recipe a long time ago. It is inspired by all the fresh seafood at the Aldo restaurant.

This dish is best using the freshest seafood you can find. You can make this dish ahead of time, since it needs to chill in the refrigerator before serving.

Court bouillon is a broth, typically used to poach foods such as seafood or vegetables.

Serving size: 2

Ingredients:

Court bouillon

    ½ gallon water

    ¼ cup white wine

    1 lemon, sliced

    1 small onion, chopped

    Salt and pepper

12 ounces total of shrimp (cleaned, peeled, and deveined with the tails removed), scallops, calamari, and octopus

2 tablespoons extra-virgin olive oil

Juice of ½ lemon

1 teaspoon minced garlic

½ teaspoon chopped chives

½ teaspoon chopped parsley

Salt and pepper

Romaine lettuce

Lemon slices

Directions:
1. Prepare the court bouillon by adding the white wine, lemon, onion and salt/pepper to taste to the water.
2. Bring the water to a boil and let it boil for about 30 minutes.
3. Add the octopus and simmer for 30 minutes.
4. Add the rest of the seafood and cook just until the shrimp turns pink, about 5 minutes.
5. Drain the seafood well and place it in a bowl.
6. Chill the seafood in the refrigerator.
7. Once the seafood is cool, remove it from the refrigerator. Slice the seafood thinly and return it to the bowl.
8. Toss the sliced seafood with the olive oil, lemon juice, garlic, chives, and parsley; season to taste with salt and pepper.
9. Serve the seafood salad on a bed of romaine lettuce with lemon slices as garnish.

Chapter 4: *Parlano la Lingua*

Speak the Language

Here I sat at an employment agency in Milan; I was twenty, and had already worked for a couple of years in the restaurant business. I felt like I was ready to take the next step in my career: working in another country.

"How could that be the next step?" someone might question. I had met several individuals who worked in various countries around Europe. Some had even worked outside Europe. Well, I listened to these people and it set my mind in motion. They had told me, "If you want to get ahead, become a host or a maître d'. That's where the money is."

The mention of more money got my attention. They told me that to become a host or maître d' at a restaurant in Europe, you need to speak more than one language. So how does that relate to me looking for working in another country? Well, the best way to learn a new language is to immerse yourself in the culture and customs of that country. Just dive into the deep end and be forced to learn the new language.

Perfecting my current job skills would not be enough to advance in the restaurant industry, I thought. Plus, the idea of moving to another country intrigued me. That's why I went to the agency in Milan and told them I was looking for a job as a waiter in another country.

The agent flicked through the relevant available positions and pulled one out. "Do you speak German?" he asked. "No, I speak just Italian. But I would like to learn German," I responded. "Well, you can't get a job as a waiter in Germany if you can't speak German. You'll have to be able to speak to and also understand the customers."

I felt momentarily deflated. The other ways to learn a language were to pay for course, which I couldn't afford, or to study on your own. Was my intended new direction already off course? Then the agent continued, and my hope returned. "But if you're willing to work as a busboy, I might have something for you. Once you learn the language, you can apply to become a waiter."

I nodded. "All right." It was a step back to work as a busboy. I felt like Sisyphus, the king from Greek mythology who was forced to roll a large boulder to the top of a hill. When Sisyphus neared the top, the boulder would roll back down to the bottom and he would have to start all over. He was condemned to this for eternity.

I had pushed the boulder up the slope in Italy only for it to roll back to the bottom in Germany. I didn't get down, though. I realized that even if I had to start over, this was potentially a step forward for me by learning a new language. Plus, it was a new type of cuisine for me to try.

"It's in the Black Forest," he explained. "It's a summer resort, so there a lot of tourists. Do you know the Black Forest?" I shook my head. It sounded mysterious and somewhat exotic.

"It's in the southwestern corner of Germany, not far from the cities of Baden-Baden and Stuttgart, near the border with France," he explained.

"It's very pretty—lots of mountains and trees. You'll travel by train. Do you have a passport?"

Again, I shook my head. This was proving to be a little more difficult. "You will need one. Here is a list of what you'll need to have before you go," he said, handing me a sheet of paper. My eyes skimmed the list of documents to get a passport: birth certificate, visa, documentation to indicate whether I had any criminal history, a physical exam, and chest x-ray…the list went on and on.

I could provide the birth certificate and visa. The criminal history? Ha. I was too busy working to get into that kind of trouble. My childhood crimes of snatching food were simply a survival mechanism for me and not an indicator of my true character. Besides, my mama's words about never stealing again had kept me on the straight and narrow. That's what drove me into the restaurant business, right? So I could satisfy my hunger and hold true to her declaration.

"You'll find instructions there on where to go for each. We can hold the position for you for a little while, but not indefinitely, so you'll need to move quickly," he added. "Do you have work certificates to document each of your prior positions?"

"Yes, except for my current job. I can ask for one there," I said, nodding. "Good. You'll need to get them and all your other documents translated into German. The German Embassy should be able to refer you to an official translator who can do that for you." Well, I had a lot of tasks to take care of now. A small price to pay for continuing my journey.

He handed me a final sheet of paper. "Here's the name and address of the hotel, along with the name and telephone number for the maître d'hôtel there. Call him when you have everything in order." I gathered the paperwork and felt a ripple of excitement as I looked at the list again. It was really happening. I was off to my next adventure.

I shook the man's hand, thanking him for the opportunity and information. I quickly strode out of the agency and into the street. I was ready to get started.

I looked around, the realization of what I was about to do hitting me. I would be leaving behind my family members living in Milan, including my baby sister, Maria. I felt in my heart that she would understand my need to continue my advancement, and she was settled in now with our sister. It would be tough. I was going to be on my own.

I would miss Milan in some ways, like I missed Cerea, but at least I had family with me then. I was striking out on my own for the first time. Severino would not be meeting me at the train station, welcoming me to my new home.

I tried not to consider that. I steeled my resolve and decided to have no regrets about taking this next step. I moved forward, applying for a copy of my birth certificate and completing most of the other requirements. I was trying to make progress. I knew that the job opening would not wait for me forever.

What I also did not know at the time was how slowly the wheels of bureaucracy moved, especially in a country like Italy. Naively, I thought that I would be able to apply for a copy of my birth certificate, obtain a passport, and get a visa simply by filling out a form or two. Then I would walk out the door with everything I needed to take the job in Germany. The documents were the key to my future.

Instead, the process dragged out. It took weeks and weeks. People in the U.S. complain about their bureaucracy—they should try to accomplish similar tasks in Italy! Finally, I had all the information in hand. But I still had to have it all translated into German. More time passed, about another couple of weeks.

I was frustrated and anxious, but I understood all this was necessary. By the time I finally had all my documents in order, I had just turned twenty-one. I placed a call to the maître d' at the hotel in Germany.

The news was not good. "I'm very sorry," the maître d' said, "but you forfeited your place because you are late." Upset, I explained the delay in gathering all the paperwork. He listened, but said unfortunately there was nothing he could do. He did promise to contact me if anything else came up.

There was nothing else I could do but return, dejected, to the employment agency in the hope that something else might be available. Before I could go back, the maître d' telephoned me. "I have something for you, but it's not in the Black Forest," he said. "It's in Frankfurt. Do you still want to come to Germany?"

I was overjoyed. I assured him that I still wanted to come. "Excellent. It's a busboy position at the Grandhotel Hessischer Hof. Write this down. I will give you the name and telephone number of the manager, and I will contact him and tell him to expect you."

This was fantastic! My plans were back on track. "How soon can you arrange to be there?" the maître d' asked. I thought about the timing, and we agreed on the date for my arrival in Frankfurt.

I gave my notice at the Ristorante Aldo, which was difficult. I really loved the Aldo and it was amazing to work there. Like I said, it was like being in a movie with all the fancily dressed people, the vibrant atmosphere, the fresh seafood. I said my goodbyes, making sure to thank everyone that had helped me.

I bought a ticket to Frankfurt on a ten o'clock in the evening train. Going back to Severino's, I went to my tiny room one last time and looked around. Pulling my suitcase out from under the bed, I placed my few belongings in. They barely filled half the case. I didn't have more leaving Milan than when I left Cerea. Keeping your life simple will never fail you.

On the bright side, my case was light enough that I could travel easily. I placed my visa, passport, train ticket, and birth certificate in the inside pocket of my jacket and put all my other documentation in my suitcase. Once I reached the station, I looked around one last time, recalling how I marveled at the sights and sounds of my arrival in Milan.

I was ready to start the next part of my journey. I boarded the train and stowed my suitcase. I looked around, finding a seat at the back of a car by the window. I settled into the seat, and prepared for the long journey to Frankfurt.

The trip would take about ten hours, as the train traveled north through Switzerland and on into central Germany. It was a pity that I would not be able to see Switzerland, as we would be passing through it in the dark. I closed my eyes and tried to sleep. The best I could manage was to doze fitfully.

I was just too excited. And, I was feeling nervous. I wasn't the least bit anxious about working at my new job, my ability to learn a new language, being away from family, or anything else at that time. I had worked my way from busboy to waiter in Italy. I was confident I could do the same in Germany once I mastered the language. Plus, I remembered my mama's words about discipline and respect. They would surely benefit me in this new endeavor.

Still, I had never experienced being unable to communicate with other people, to speak or understand them. Now, I would be surrounded by people who spoke a different language. I wasn't sure how different it would be from Italian.

Not only that, but what customs and mannerisms were different between Germany and Italy? What about taboos in this new land? The restaurant business in Italy required an exacting approach to serving diners. How would working in a restaurant in Germany differ? I also wondered if the German people I met would be patient with me.

How would these citizens of a big city like Frankfurt treat me, an Italian from the countryside.

Also, keep in mind that this was less than two decades after the end of World War II. I thought back to all that I had heard about the Germans after the war. Germany and Italy were technically allies for a while. Then Italy tried to surrender to the Allies and Germany stepped in to prevent our country from switching sides. The blood of German troops had spilled in the Italian earth. Germans bombs, like the one that injured my sister, had fallen on us. Ultimately, the relationship had not gone well.

I thought about the German soldiers I had met during the war and the way they shared their rations with us, trying to help us however they could. My experience was generally positive, but how would the soldiers I met during wartime differ from the civilians in peacetime?

Would the German populace harbor any ill will about the war and its outcome? Did they hold a grudge? What would the people be like in general, and would they accept me? So many questions, but I hoped the answers—one way or another—would come quickly.

At that point, I shook myself and thought *It doesn't matter. None of it matters, because I will make it. I am going to learn German, no matter what it takes. I will use discipline and respect to help me fit in.* I was sure that my approach would take me far.

At eight the next morning, the train rolled into the Frankfurt station. I collected my suitcase and followed the stream of people getting off the train. Joining the queue for international passengers, I patiently waited for my turn. I looked around, and was once again struck by the hustle and bustle of the station, such a contrast to our sleepy little station back home.

After weeks and weeks of gathering all the required documentation, I was here. Presenting it to the border officer proved to be quite anticlimactic. He spoke fluent Italian, reviewed everything, and asked me a number of questions. Everything was in order and he was satisfied with my answers. He handed all the documents back to me and bid me good luck with my new job. That was it. I was now officially in Germany. My first time to live outside my homeland.

I asked where I could change some of my precious, hard-earned lire into deutschmarks and he pointed the way to a place I could make the exchange. I made my way through the immense station, looking around excitedly like the young boy from Cerea. I just took it all in.

Wow, I kept repeating to myself, as my eyes stopped on one thing after another. The station looked like a palace with lights blazing everywhere. It was teeming with people. The conversations that surrounded me were unintelligible. The sounds were all so… foreign! It wasn't just the words that were strange to me. The rhythm, the cadence was different from anything I'd ever heard before in Italy. I couldn't read the signs around the station, either.

It was a disconcerting feeling. I truly was a stranger in a strange land. The proverbial *pesce* out of water. I felt like one of the unfortunate inhabitants of the Aldo's seafood offering. I took a deep breath and realized I didn't care. I was happy to be in Germany.

I handed my lire to the clerk, sad to see them go. They represented my home. I tried not to feel dismayed at the few deutschmarks I received in exchange. He said something to me that I didn't understand. I shrugged, my confusion evident. He scribbled something down on a piece of paper and shoved it at me. I guess he was used to dealing with foreigners. The paper read "1 DM = 156 lire." I learned a lesson in commerce and economics that day, how the value of one country's money differed greatly from another's.

I nodded at the clerk, still feeling a bit bewildered. I feared that I might have been shortchanged. Would I even have enough for a taxi, or would I have to walk? Then it occurred to me that the hotel could help me if I didn't have enough money.

Feeling reassured, I looked around and made my way to an exit. I pressed through the surge of humanity. Stepping out from the station to the streets of Frankfurt, I paused. No one to greet me. No familiar faces, obviously. The mayor of Frankfurt and a band were not waiting outside to welcome me (not that I was really expecting them); on the other hand, a lynch mob wasn't forming. Everyone around me was merely indifferent.

The city was different than Milan, yet similar too. The faces definitely looked different. The buildings and architecture were different. But there was an energy and sense of purpose to the people as they hurried about the streets. It was a similar vibe to Milan.

Frankfurt was bombed heavily by the Americans and British during World War II, but the city had been undergoing a revitalization following the end of the war (as was the rest of the country). After growing up in Italy, where so many of the buildings were extremely old, Frankfurt was glistening and new.

Untold millions of dollars had arrived from the U.S. as part of the Marshall Plan, helping to rebuild Germany after the war. Many modern buildings had been built to replace the older ones destroyed by bombs. Like Milan, it was had developed into a center of commerce and finance during its long history. Various trades and arts flourished in the city, as well.

I held tight to the piece of paper with the hotel's name and address. I had no idea where or how far away it was, so I began looking for a taxi. "Taxi, taxi!" I shouted, waving when I spied one. I was lucky. The word *Taxi* is the same in Italian as German (as well as English and Spanish, and other languages). So, I had a new German word for my vocabulary.

The driver pulled up alongside me. I jumped in, putting my lightweight suitcase with all my possessions on the floor next to my feet. The driver said something to me that I didn't understand. I presumed he was asking my destination. I looked at the paper in my hand. "Hôtel Hessischer Hof," I said, trying (and failing) to blend in and sound like I spoke the least bit of German.

He pulled away from the curb and only a minute later pulled up in front of the hotel. The hotel, it turned out, was only a quarter of a mile from the station. I could have walked! Oh well, you live and learn. To be safe on the safe side I offered him the largest banknote I had. I was relieved when he gave me change. Thanking him, I hopped out of the taxi and looked at the hotel.

The hotel was located near the historical center of the city. It was owned, I'd been told, by counts and princes from the German state of Hesse. Hesse was its own country before the German Reich had been formed in the 1870s.

It was, and still is, a fine hotel. Konrad Adenauer, elected in 1949 as the first Chancellor of the Federal Republic of Germany, frequently stayed at the hotel. The hotel interior was opulent without being excessive. Impressive paintings hung on every wall, but it was the antique furniture that caught my eye. I knew enough from that first job in Milan to recognize the quality of the pieces.

A bellman intercepted me as I stepped inside. He picked up my suitcase and escorted me to the front desk. The man behind the front desk greeted me. "I am here to see your maître d'hôtel," I said in Italian. He and the bellman looked at me, and then each other. *"Der Maître d'hôtel?"* the man at the desk said. I don't know if he understood Italian, but at least he picked up that I wanted to see the maître d'.

The bellman, realizing I was not actually a guest, abruptly dropped my suitcase and retreated without a word. *Remember Carlo, discipline and respect. It wasn't you personally.* I guess it was to be expected. He knew he wasn't getting a tip from me, not if I was going to be a fellow hotel staff member.

The man behind the desk picked up the telephone and spoke into it. More words I didn't understand. A few minutes later, a man entered the reception area, glanced around, and met my gaze. He walked up to me and shook my hand.

"I've been waiting for you," he said, in Italian. That made me feel much better. He summoned an employee and gave him some instructions. Turning back to me, he said, "He will show you to your room in the dormitory, where you can leave your suitcase. He will get you a uniform, so get changed and come back here. You will begin work immediately."

Well, no wasting time here, a very efficient process. After all those months of waiting to get my paperwork and get here, I started work right away. My nervous expectations and questions about my arrival in this new land dissolved. I was accepted for what I was. A busboy from Italy working at a restaurant in Germany. No dramatic situation at the hotel front desk.

The hotel provided modest accommodations and meals for the staff, however these were not free. We were charged one mark a day out of our salary of forty marks every month. At the time, a mark was worth about twenty-five cents in the U.S. back then. Although twenty-five cents for room and board in the early '60s was not a kingly sum, I was left with very little money afterwards. I had maybe ten marks to last the entire month.

I did not pay any attention to how what my salary would be when I was offered the job. Like an eager kid, I was focused on one thing. All that was on my mind was that I was there to learn German. It was all part of the plan: learn another language, discover another culture in the process, and eventually move up to host or maître d' in the business.

I wondered what my mama would think about her little boy, leaving Cerea, leaving Italy, and planning bigger things for myself. I felt that she would allow herself a moment of pride in my accomplishments so far, before reminding me I still had far to go.

I knew I was going to having to take a demotion back to busboy, and suffer through that start from the bottom again. I was prepared for that, at least, until I could speak the language. For now, I reminded myself I was investing in me and my future. The dividends on that investment would come later. I would make sure of that.

A busboy's job is pretty much the same, be it in Italy, Germany, England, or wherever. You serve from the left and clear from the right. All the other associated tasks were familiar to me as well.

It was the waiter's job to take the customer's order, which required knowing the language. From Day One in Frankfurt, I had a goal: to learn the language. As I had at my previous jobs, I would immerse myself in the environment and soak up as much knowledge as I could. I vowed to be persistent in my efforts to learn the language.

My room in the staff dormitory, my first outside of my family home or my brother's house, was tiny. It was like a railway berth and was nothing more than a single bed and a small closet. I could hardly turn around once I got inside. It didn't matter though, I would only be there to sleep. I would spend all my non-working hours outside the hotel, sightseeing around Frankfurt and trying to learn German.

Shoving my suitcase under the bed, I quickly donned my new uniform. Quickly, I headed to the dining room. The maître d' wasted no time and explained my duties to me. He gave me a cursory tour of the kitchen then the dining areas. He informed me there were staff meetings every few months, where he would review policy and procedures with us.

The dining room menu consisted mostly of fish, lamb, and pork. I would help carry the food on silver trays from the kitchen to a side table for final preparation by the waiter, as was the tradition in first-class European restaurants. The waiter would debone the fish or carve the meat, plate it, and present it to each customer. If it was a dish with a sauce, the chefs would assemble the plate in the kitchen.

Overall, I was discovered that I was not too fond of German food in general. Everything was very heavy, like dumplings, gravies, and stews. I preferred the lighter ingredients of Italian cooking. I did discover a couple of German dishes that I liked: Schweinshaxe (roasted pig shank) and a roasted lamb.

The only difference between this and the fine restaurants I worked at in Milan was that in Germany, everything was more precise, more disciplined, and a bit more rigid. That was okay. I appreciated learning the new skills.

Learning the language, however, proved far more difficult. I heard my mother's words in my head again, *disciplina, rispetto*. I scoured bookstores for a German/Italian dictionary. I found a copy and parted with some the few deutschmarks I had after paying the required fee for room and meals. The book would be a good start. It wouldn't necessarily teach me syntax, verb conjugation, and other aspects of learning a new language, but at least I could start adding some words to my limited vocabulary.

As I walked around Frankfurt in my free time, I would write down the words I saw on signs. Once again, a notebook was a useful tool for me. Using the dictionary, I would look the words up from the signs I had seen and jot down the translations. I did the same with newspapers, and I eventually progressed towards working my way through a book. My reading materials were another expense, but an investment in me.

It was slow going and my translation dictionary was getting a good workout, as was my brain. German isn't at all like Italian. It has a different root language than Italian, which is considered a romance language along with others such as French and Spanish. I had to learn all new words and rules.

After about five months, I looked into taking language classes to speed up my progress. Although I wasn't spending my money on much of anything outside of reading materials to help with my language skills, with just ten extra marks to my name per month, the courses were still too expensive.

Occasionally, I would spend a little money on watching movies. I understood next to nothing of the movie; however, it was a way to immerse myself in the language. I would try to follow a story, to see whether I could pick out words I had already learned, and try to learn a few more. I think I annoyed the audience members around me, asking "What did he say? What does that mean?" I would concentrate so intensely that I would come out of the theater each time with a headache.

One of the first and most important phrases I first learned to say, and definitely over-used, was "How do you say this? How do you say that?" Everyone I met was really patient with me and willing to help me learn. (I think the theater goers might not have appreciated my effort to learn during a movie, though). My co-workers would say, "No, Carlo, you don't say it like that. You say it like *this*!" They helped me a lot with my pronunciation.

So, I spent virtually all my free time with my nose in my dictionary, learning German. This was key to fitting in here in Germany. I was determined to make a career, and a life, in my new country. And even though I had only completed second grade, I was determined to be a good student now and learn as much knowledge and new skills as I could. As long as I stayed on the path and didn't get sidetracked, that is.

A few of my co-workers invited me along with them on a trip about thirty minutes west to Wiesbaden. They didn't tell me where we were going. Well, it turned out they wanted to go to the Wiesbaden Casino, one of the oldest in Germany.

As soon as I found out what they were going to do, I was mortified. My thoughts quickly flashed to the story of how my father had gambled away his inheritance. I wanted nothing to do with gambling. So, I found something else to entertain myself while they gambled and drank.

Another time, one of the waiters who I was friendly with asked me to go out for a beer. "You have to try the German beer," my friend insisted. "It's the best in the world." My co-worker hailed from Spain and since Spanish and Italian are similar enough, we could understand each other (mostly).

I had never had a beer before; as an Italian, I drank wine. I agreed anyway, and we headed off to get a beer together. I wanted to understand the culture as well as the language. Beer is to Germany as wine is to Italy, no?

We found a bar, settled down, and ordered. The bartender returned, placing an enormous glass of the amber liquid in front of me. "It's a half-liter," my friend said, which equals about seventeen ounces.

I took a sip. Smacking my lips, I exclaimed, "Oh, that's very good." He clinked his glass against mine and said, "Drink up!" I did just that. I enjoyed it so much that I downed the entire glass in about a minute.

"You want another one?" I nodded, and he ordered me another one. After three of these huge glasses in a short amount of time, I was hopelessly drunk. My friend had to help me walk home. Luckily, we were fairly close to our dormitory because we couldn't afford to take the bus.

I began vomiting and was sick for two days. During that time, I could barely sleep. There was a flashing neon sign outside my window with no shutter or curtain to block the harsh light. The light tormented me during my inebriated state, flicking on and off over and over again. I hated that light.

I was so exhausted and ill, I could barely drag myself out of my bedroom to the bathroom. "So much for respect and discipline," I groaned. And so much for my pledge to never drink so much again after my first day in Milan.

I almost got fired when I didn't show up for work the next day. My partner in crime, who could hold his liquor better than me, confessed the whole situation to our boss, "Carlo is not coming to work this morning. We went out last night and he got really drunk. He's been throwing up all night."

When I dragged myself in to work two days later, I was pale and subdued. I went up to my boss and sheepishly said, "I'm so sorry. This has never happened before and I promise it will never happen again." He looked at me. I expected fireworks. Instead, he calmly said "Well, I hope you learned your lesson."

He was extremely understanding about it; I soon learned that most Germans aren't surprised when somebody gets drunk. I could have lost my job, but thanks to my boss and his willingness to let me slide on my infraction, I didn't.

I had worked hard to get where I was. I certainly didn't want to get in trouble and fired. I swore to myself then that I would never, ever drink beer again. Only wine. Even though I was living in Germany, I was still Italian.

Even though I felt like I had a momentary lapse by getting drunk and momentarily lapsing on my credo of respect and discipline, one of my co-workers set a bad example of how to act in a different culture. He got drunk and picked a fight with some of the locals. At work the next day, his face was cut and his eye was swollen. As I looked at him, I knew that was something I would not, could not, ever do. I wanted to blend into my new home, not stand out by fighting.

Despite my pledge to never drink beer again, I still drank wine. A good host or maître d' knows wine. To know wine, you have to taste it. You must be able to describe its taste and make recommendations. I had learned my lesson though, so I only would drink wine in moderation.

One day, the hotel hosted a reception by the Portuguese Chamber of Commerce. At the time, I didn't realize what an impact the country of Portugal would have on my life. My future wife would be a Portuguese national and I would lose a significant amount of money investing in the country's real estate market.

The event was to promote one of Portugal's most popular exports, Port wine, coming into Germany. They invited celebrities and journalists, as well as their target audience, the German people.

The hotel had the staff wear tuxedos. I had dressed nicely for my many jobs, but I had never actually worn a tuxedo before. The tables were draped in elegant tablecloths that fell to the floor, topped with crystal candelabras and floral centerpieces. Those tables were soon to be laden with every imaginable hors d'oeuvre on silver platters, to pair with and showcase the legendary fortified wine.

We filed into the reception room an hour before it was scheduled to start. I was taken aback by how many bottles there were. I have never seen so much Port in my life! "Okay guys, open everything," the maître d' said.

We looked at each other, startled. Everything? There were easily more than a hundred bottles, with vintages ranging from 1948 all the way back to 1850. "Let me show you how," the maître d' said. "You have to be exceedingly careful not to break the corks. The corks can be soft, especially in some of the really old bottles." Obviously, it was bad if bits of cork fell into the bottle then ended up in the guests' glasses.

After all the bottles had been carefully opened, the maître d' stepped out of the room. We looked at each other, then at the bottles. All that Port was just too tempting. We had to grab this rare opportunity and see what all the fuss was about.

It was part of my education, I said to myself, justifying what I was about to do. That way, when I became a waiter, I can speak knowingly by having tried it. We couldn't risk being caught, though, or we would surely be reprimanded, possibly even fired. I already felt like I was on thin ice with the boss for the previous alcohol-related incident.

One of the waiters had a solution for us to sip the Port in private. He lifted up a tablecloth. "Go under the table and I'll pass you a glass," he told us. One by one, we crawled under the table and tasted the Port. It was good, surprisingly fruity and faintly sweet, but strong in terms of alcohol. I was glad I had taken the opportunity to try it. I felt like a little kid though, sneaking a taste of wine without a parent finding out.

When the reception ended four hours later, a considerable amount of Port remained. The maître d'hôtel said he was really pleased at how well everything went. He praised us for how smoothly and attentively we had all done our jobs.

"Okay, guys, great job. As a reward, each of you can take one bottle of Port with you." There were twelve of us and we did not hesitate to grab a bottle. I remember taking a bottle of 1948.

As I said, I learned my lesson about drinking, or at least drinking beer. I decided I should drink wine sparingly, and with a special wine like the Port, savor it slowly or enjoy it on special occasions. So I drank no more than a few sips of the '48 Port every month, as a treat for myself. I finished the last of it after I moved to England, four years later. Talk about making it last.

Honestly, I enjoyed my job. Even the new tasks came to me naturally enough. As a busboy, I had to clear dishes, napkins, glasses, and flatware off each table after those guests had left, then reset the table for the next party. In English, my latest adopted language, this is referred to as "turning the tables."

This was not always exciting work, but I was hungry to learn and ready to add new skills and knowledge to my existing ones. I came to intuitively understand that achieving this turnaround rapidly and efficiently was vital to restaurant operations. I took this lesson to heart and filed this knowledge away for future reference.

This simple process is essential to making a restaurant or hotel dining room not only efficient, but profitable. The more guests you are able to serve, the more cash flow. Basic economics. Many of today's restaurants take this approach to the extreme, rushing guests through their meals just to get the next ones seated. The dining experience is harried and not pleasant for the guests.

I would teach my staff how to turn the tables quickly when I operated my own restaurant, but with a twist. As I mentioned previously, my technique was to invite guests to the bar for a drink or dessert. They loved it! They didn't feel rushed, but it freed up the table. I would make up the cost of the dessert or drink by getting the next party served.

An additional perk of being a busboy, as I saw it, was going in and out of the kitchen. This German cuisine was so different from any version of Italian cuisine. I always kept a curious eye on what the chefs and cooks were doing to turn out dishes. I looked with the eyes of waiter, not a busboy.

This approach had worked for me in Italy, and it worked for me here. If I hadn't carefully watched what was going on in the kitchen, how would I know what the food looked like going out to the guests? As a busboy, I would only see the scattered remnants or empty plates once the guests had finished with each course.

We typically worked inside the restaurant, but sometimes we handled a wedding or other big event at a castle owned by the family of the hotel owners. The castle was about twenty miles outside Frankfurt. It was luxurious. Anyone who has seen a movie about any royals or pictures of castles can imagine the setting. The castle would come back into my mind years later when I visited the shimmering residence of French kings at Versailles while on vacation.

I would dress in a tuxedo with tails, helping with these upscale events. It was all part of restaurant theater. The crème de la crème attended these social occasions, and I was there among them, practicing discipline and respect. Little Carlo from Cerea.

My family would be amazed if they knew where I was. I had gone from my tiny, rural village in Italy to a grand castle in Germany. My sweet mama said she saw great things for me and I was getting there. I was still learning the language and getting acclimated to the culture, but I started to feel that restlessness tug at me again.

At the time, I wasn't sure why I was always on the move, switching jobs, yearning to learn more and more new things. Eventually, I would have a realization about this drive in me, but for now I didn't think much about this as I cast my eyes in a new direction. I had heard about a new restaurant in Frankfurt that intrigued me.

My special recipe for you: Rack of Lamb Provençal

Obviously, I grew up eating nothing but homemade Italian food during my childhood. I didn't experience any dishes or cooking styles from other cultures until I moved to Germany. Many of these dishes were really different than what I was used to, such as sauerkraut and bratwurst.

Some vaguely reminded me of Italian dishes, such as schnitzel (milanesa style of thin, breaded meat) and spaetzle (egg noodle pasta), but they didn't compare to their distant Italian cousins in my mind.

The types of dishes that appealed to me the most were ones featuring roasted meats, such as pork and lamb. Here is a recipe in the spirit of the roasted lamb dishes that I ate during time my time in Germany.

Serving size: 2

Ingredients:

1 ½-lb. rack of lamb

Dijon mustard (enough to spread thinly all over lamb)

½ cup bread crumbs (garlic, parsley, salt pepper, oregano, and butter, spread on baguette and baked until brown; grate the bread to create your own breadcrumbs)

Butter (1 tablespoon drizzled on breadcrumbs after you spread it on the lamb)

½ tablespoon Italian parsley

3 tablespoons extra-virgin olive oil

Salt and pepper

Directions:

1. Trim the fat off the lamb.
2. Finely chop the parsley.
3. In a bowl, combine the bread crumbs and parsley, then add salt and pepper to taste.
4. In a stainless steel, oven-safe pan, heat the olive oil over medium heat.
5. When the oil is hot, sear the lamb on both sides.
6. In a separate skillet, heat the butter until melted. Add the bread crumb mixture to the butter and stir to combine.

7. Pour the bread crumb and butter mixture over the lamb; make sure all sides of the lamb are coated.

8. Place the lamb in the oven at 350 degrees and cook it for 10 minutes until (about 160 degrees for medium); the bread crumb coating should be brown.

9. Slice the lamb. Serve with sautéed vegetables or roasted potatoes.

Chapter 5:

Casa è Dove Si Rendono

Home is Where You Make it

Seven months after I had begun working at the hotel, a waiter told me about another restaurant in Frankfurt. The restaurant, called Weinhaus Brückenkeller, was not far away from the hotel, on Schützenstrasse.

As the name Weinhaus indicates, the Brückenkeller included a sizable wine cellar. The place had originally opened as beer hall and only later became a restaurant, earning quite a gastronomic reputation before World War II. It was destroyed during the bombing by the Allies, but rebuilt and reopened, like other buildings in Frankfurt.

The restaurant was cozy and seated no more than a hundred people at most. The restaurant had most of its space dedicated to storing its massive wine collection. The old wine barrels were so enormous that one of them was used as a changing room for the musicians who strolled through the dining room, playing for the customers. I really liked the look and feel of the wine cellar atmosphere and would later use it as inspiration for my restaurant's wine cellar.

This was the early 1960s and the Cold War gripped the world. Germany was divided between West and East after the Allied forces had driven through the country in

World War II. Now, the former Allies that defeated the Axis powers were divided by an "Iron Curtain" with the U.S. on one side and the Soviets the other.

The U.S. had troops stationed throughout Germany to counter the Soviet threat of invasion from East Germany. Near Frankfurt, there was a U.S. Army base in Friedberg. Elvis Presley was one of the soldiers stationed there during his military service. Because he was a major star before he got drafted into the Army, he was able to live off-base in a hotel.

My waiter friend who told me about the Brückenkeller claimed it had been Elvis's favorite place to dine. If it was good enough for the King of Rock and Roll, it was good enough for us. So along with a friend of mine from Spain, we went to apply. A few weeks had passed before someone from the restaurant staff called to say they had places for us. We gave notice to the hotel restaurant right away and departed for our new jobs at the end of the month.

I knew I didn't have the language skills yet to be a waiter, so I got a job as a busboy, again. The climb to the next step in my career required great patience on my part. This would be a chance to learn a different style of service, though. I was excited to get started.

It must have been exciting to be working at the restaurant and have Elvis dining there. Elvis had completed his military service and had returned home by the time I started, but I was admittedly curious to potentially see other celebrities dine at the restaurant. I didn't know if I would see any on the level of Elvis, since the King was on a level of his own. However, I still wanted to see them for myself.

Like I've said, my life in Milan and Germany was like a movie in many ways: grand locations, elegantly dressed people, and plenty of action. However, the movie was more likely to star Grace Kelly and Cary Grant than the cowboys I had grown up watching. If a cowboy walked into one of these restaurants, I think everyone would have fainted.

We would occasionally serve celebrities at the Brückenkeller. That's what the waiters all talked about, especially those who'd been on duty back in 1959 when Elvis would eat there. They said Elvis never dined alone. He was always seated with three or four other people. The other waiters would nudge his server and urge him to ask the star to get up and perform. "Hey, Giovanni, why don't you ask him to sing for us? Tell him, come on and get up."

Of course, Elvis was a customer at the restaurant, just a guest seeking to enjoy his meal and relax. It wasn't as if he would ever get up and entertain the crowd. He was there on his nights off, trying to keep a low profile during his service. I was told Elvis took his soldiering seriously, lest anyone think he was receiving extraordinary treatment. I heard he'd even won medals for marksmanship; he would be fascinated by guns throughout his life. He also picked up karate during his time in the service, which he later incorporated into his stage performances.

Although I enjoyed seeing celebrities and powerful people in the restaurant where worked, I would always treat them as regular customers. I've been around movie stars, musicians, CEOs of major corporations, and politicians. Over the years of my restaurant career, so many people have wondered why I didn't get these famous people to sign items or pose for a picture. My answer? Always the same: I treated them as if they were any other customer. I would never ask for autographs, and taking a photograph was a huge no-no.

Well, back to reality. While the rich and famous could afford to dine in the places I worked, I could not. Money was still very tight on a busboy's wages. When the opportunity arose for me to work short term as a dishwasher after my regular shift, I leaped at the chance. I still hoped I could afford to take some formal German language courses.

As I walked past restaurants in my sightseeing trips around the city, I would look into the windows and dream of the day I could go inside and eat dinner. I could afford treating myself to ice cream every once in a while, though. I found a place that served the most amazing frozen dairy concoctions. It was different than gelato, Italian-style ice cream, which contains less fat and air than ice cream.

This place used all fresh ingredients, buying milk straight from the dairy farm with a lot of butter fat. The fruits and nuts were all from local sources, as well. The ice cream was totally decadent. It was so popular, the locals would line up even during winter to eat it.

Along with the ability to pay for language classes, it would be nice to have some extra money to eat out or go to a disco. I found a second job. The Brückenkeller was only open for dinner, so I would finish my shift at ten o'clock in the evening. I would then relax for a while before working as a dishwasher from midnight until three o'clock in the morning at another place, Picasso Keller; it was a popular nightclub in the city. I did this for two straight months.

When I finally had saved enough, I decide to spend the money on the German lessons I had long sought, along with two friends of mine, one from Bologna in Italy and the other from Seville in Spain. My little group understood we couldn't earn more money until we could speak the language. We also needed money to learn the language. I would later learn to call that a Catch-22. My life, personally and professionally, had been, and would be, filled with Catch-22s

The lessons were far more important to me than going out to eat or hanging out at a club. The notion of spending my hard-earned extra cash on extravagances crossed my mind, but my mama's confidence in me won out. One day, my friends and I went together to the Johann Wolfgang University.

We began filling out an application for German language classes. I skimmed through the information searching for the bottom line, the fees. I found them. Wow, I was stunned. "How can we afford this?" I asked my friends. They shrugged. We had enough money to attend eight lessons, but not enough for a full course aimed at fluency. That was the plan, now.

I was excited to learn as much as I could, though. Despite this short-term enrollment, the school was excellent and I knew we would learn a lot. Oh my God, I thought, I'm going to school. Me, who hadn't been to school since I was seven years old. I was going back to school to learn German.

We went twice a week to the university, two hours at a time, for four weeks. I was learning so many new things about the language, and studying as hard as I could in my free time. I was so enthusiastic about being a student again! My mama would be proud.

Unfortunately, my time at school passed quickly and the eight lessons were done. It made me sad; even though I knew I could no longer continue, I became much more determined to learn the language. Every free minute I had, I would walk around the city to learn on the streets. I would read the signs and listen to conversations, trying to pick out a word here or there. I would sit down somewhere and write, translate, and practice speaking the language.

Fortunately, I found a new place to be studious, to sit and learn. And even better, someone to help me. Her name was Frau Schultz. Since I had left my employment at the hotel, I had to move out of the dormitory and find a new place to live. My new employer did not provide accommodations for the restaurant staff. One of my co-workers had mentioned a lady, a war widow, who occasionally would rent out a room in her home.

That is how I came to know Frau Schultz. She was a nice, very matronly and caring woman, probably in her early to mid-fifties, and of solid German stock. She would make me breakfast, joining me at the table as I dug into a hearty meal of sausage, eggs, and bread. She would ask me how my language skills were progressing. Between mouthfuls of food, I would respond as best as possible. She would patiently listen and help me as I worked to learn both the spoken and written language.

No one had cared for me since my mother passed away like Frau Schultz did. I soon came to consider her as a second mother to me. It was something that I needed at that time. I was far from home, working for meager wages, and struggling to learn the language. My progress was slow. I just needed someone to keep me true to my path.

I'm sure the explorers of old reached some point along their journey where the situation looked bleak, home far behind them, the headwinds fighting them, the seas roiling below them, the driving rain stinging them. Above their heads, the clouded skies obscured the stars, defeating any chance of navigating through the raging storm to golden shores.

I never doubted my destination and my ability to get there; I just really needed those clouds to part so I could find my North Star. Essentially, it was time for me to become comfortable with my adopted language so I could advance in my quest.

Frau Schultz appeared in my life to guide me to that goal. It was like my mama knew and arranged for me to meet my kindly landlord and new supporter. I felt that Frankfurt and Frau Schultz's boarding house was as close to home as I had in a while.

I lived in Frau Schultz's home for almost two years, with her feeding me and working on my language skills. I was determined to learn the language. *Persistenza* (persistence) was one of my stronger traits; it had gotten me this far. I was not giving up on this new language.

One day, it was like the thick fog had passed and the sun broke through. I was speaking to a stranger, I remember, and realized I had understood what he had said without having to try to consciously translate it. I will never forget how excited I felt. I knew then that I was on my way toward getting a job as a waiter. Frau Schultz was pleased to play a part in me learning the language.

Being able to speak and understand German paid off. With my new language skills, I was finally able to apply for a waiter's position. I left the Brückenkeller and found a temporary job at a restaurant in the airport, subbing for a waiter who was out sick. I worked there for about a month when the waiter (a fellow Italian, from Naples) came back to reclaim his position. I was then out of work. It was a good job, and I wished that I could continue to work there.

No matter. I soon landed a job as a waiter at the Restaurant Börsenkeller. I was now earning three or four times what I had earned as a busboy! Another step on my path. It was an important time for me. All my hard work to learn German was paying off with a better salary.

I could afford eating out some times, and I went to a few more movies to practice my comprehension skills. Things were looking up for me. But the world was about to change around me.

Europe and the world had gone from a worldwide conflict between the Allies and Axis powers to a Cold War between the superpowers of the U.S. and U.S.S.R. A young, charismatic U.S. President, John F. Kennedy, was invigorating the free world with his vigor and confidence. West Germans flocked by the thousands to catch a glimpse of the handsome President as he visited their country in summer of 1963, in a show of unity and support between the two countries.

In June 1963, Kennedy came to speak to the citizens of Frankfurt before heading to Berlin, where he delivered his famous *"Ich bin ein Berliner"* speech. I joined the cheering throng of people who lined the streets to watch his motorcade come by. I watched with excitement as his limousine passed by, and I caught a glimpse of JFK. My friend raised his camera to snap a blurry photo of the car.

Later that year, in November, I was leaving a movie when I saw someone reading a newspaper. I saw the headline, stopping in my tracks and trying to comprehend what I had just read. I couldn't believe it. The President had been shot and killed. Who could do such a thing? Why? My mind raced, thinking back to that summer day when I and the crowd around me had jammed together to just see JFK for a few brief moments. I felt like I had lost a family member.

It was so tragic that he was gone, I thought. His death caused a strong reaction in me. JFK had died way too early, his life cut short with those shots in Dallas. My dear mama had passed away so quickly as well; one moment she and I were preparing the ingredients for the family meal and the next she was being buried.

I thought of the President and his family, his wife Jackie and two young children Caroline and John. Irish Catholic is not all that different from Italian Catholic. He had a big family with a number of brothers and sisters. He was a great man and admired by millions around the world. So many people looked up to him, and he inspired so many of them to do amazing things.

I thought of my family, my mama and my siblings. In my small world, my mama had encouraged and challenged me to get where I was today, to reach for goals that took me beyond Cerea. My father? He didn't do a thing for anyone other than himself. Well, he did motivate me to leave.

Around me, the German people were all shocked by JFK's assassination. They all felt a true connection to the young American and reacted deeply to his death. Many wept openly in the streets. Businesses came to a halt. News outlets replayed coverage of his recent visit to Germany. Life was at a standstill.

I wondered what would happen to Germany now. Kennedy supported the country and its people, not blinking in the stare down with the Soviets. Would the Soviets take advantage of the President's death? Only time would tell. Our grief mixed with uncertainty and concern.

Days and months passed, and the sting and heartbreak of the earth-shattering event began to ease. The political situation did not vary much and the mood of the people eventually returned to normal. Life would continue. But it would never be the same.

I thought about simpler times and my boyhood in Cerea. The world always got in my way, whether it was bombs raining down on me and my family during the war or cancer striking down my beloved mama. I didn't let that deter me though. They were obstacles to overcome, the unknown parts of the maps the Italian explorers of long ago sought to chart. I had a path in mind and intended to stick to it, no matter what I faced.

Now though, I decided to make the path a little easier to travel. I fondly recalled the freedom provided by my yellow bike, purchased by my mama with the funds she labored to stash away and keep secret from my father. I missed that bike, and how it allowed me to get around sleepy little Cerea. I thought about how I had to walk everywhere before my bike, and how my shoes were always falling apart.

I finally decided that I'd had enough walking around Frankfurt, especially in the cold and rain. I was ready to buy my first car. With my waiter's salary, I could afford an inexpensive one now. Not only would a car make it easier to go where I needed for work but it also opened up possibilities for exploring around Germany whenever I had a day off.

I purchased a small sporty Italian car, a Fiat 500. I was moving up in the world, and all it took was learning to speak German. For three months, the car and I were inseparable. We were made for each other. I would drive to work, out of the elements, and give my feet a rest. Restaurant workers spend a lot of time on their feet and I was able to get a brief respite behind the wheel of my Fiat.

Well, my days with the car were numbered. After having it for only three short months, a lady taking her new Mercedes for a drive ran a stop sign and plowed into my beautiful little car on the driver's side. This was to be my first of over twenty-five accidents. I've said it and will repeat it: I love cars, but they don't love me.

I realized I was lucky and could have been killed in the accident. I only suffered a few scratches, but my poor car was not as lucky. It was totaled. The police filled out their report, the insurance gave me a cash settlement, and the Fiat left my life as quickly as I entered it.

I needed some new wheels. I decided, then and there, that driving was a bit too dangerous in such a small car. The Fiat was too tiny, compared to many of the German cars on the road. So, I basically bought a tank: the much larger and stronger Opal Captain. I had my freedom again, along with protection. I'm certain the vehicle saved my life when I was involved in a terrible crash three and a half years later in Brie, France.

When you're faced with your own mortality, as when you've been in a car accident, you sometimes think about your life. As your past "flashes before your eyes," you evaluate what has gone right or wrong, what you might change, what opportunities you missed, and the actions you regret or words left unsaid.

You might look at my resume from those years and think I wasn't happy. I changed jobs so many times. But actually, the opposite was almost always true. I loved my work, I loved the business, I just about always enjoyed my co-workers, and I respected my bosses.

I knew I was on the right path, and my aim was to learn as many new skills and gain as much knowledge as I could. I wasn't alone in this quest. There was actually a terrific network in Frankfurt among all the foreign waiters and restaurant staff. We were from all over: Italy, Spain, Turkey, and many other nationalities. Most of my co-workers were like me, from countries much poorer than Germany.

That was the nature of labor in Europe in those days, and to some degree it's the nature of labor anywhere. People travel from poorer countries to richer ones for opportunities they can't find at home. In the process, they learn a new language as best they can and seek out new job skills. They start the difficult climb up the ladder to some form of success, as they define it. I can promise you, it's not an easy climb at all.

A critical part of that success is learning and knowledge. To advance, to make better wages, you must learn. And continue to learn. Which is what I was doing, inspired by my mama and aided by people like Frau Schultz.

I didn't realize it at the time, but I was using work and the opportunities to learn new things that it offered as a substitute— a substitute for the schooling my father had ripped away from me those many years ago.

I never fully understood this until decades later when I had become a boss myself. Once I came to this realization though, I was surprised I hadn't made the connection sooner. My father made me go to work instead of class when I was only seven. Something inside me must have understood that I needed to make up for my lack of schooling by taking new jobs and striving to learn something from each one.

My every experience, with every situation and new person I met, became my classroom. Work was my education beyond the second grade. There was nothing my father could do to take that away from me now. My knowledge and skills were building as I marched on my journey.

So here in Germany, my new adopted home, I had broken away from my past and continued to plot a course for my next destination. I had learned the language, worked hard to integrate into the culture, and gained valuable knowledge of the restaurant business; I did this through respect and discipline, those words my mama had told me in our home in the countryside. Those words had taken me far. I had left home and found a new one.

My special recipe for you: Cassata

Cassata is a sweet treat in Italy. However, there are two different versions. One is a sponge cake-style dessert soaked with liqueur or fruit juice with layers of ricotta cheese and candied fruit. The other version is a Neapolitan-style ice cream with nuts and dried fruit.

To me, cassata is an ice cream dish. This makes it relevant to my time in Germany, as I frequently enjoyed some of the freshest ice cream I've ever had. The place I would go was always busy, even in winter.

Here is my salute to ice cream, Italian style. This version is simple yet tasty and makes a sweet ending to a romantic dinner.

Serving size: 4

Ingredients:

1 pint each of high-quality vanilla, strawberry, and pistachio ice cream

1 tablespoon walnuts (finely crushed)

1 tablespoon pistachios (finely crushed)

Raisins (chopped; red, white, or mixed)

1 tablespoon maraschino liqueur (or rum)

3 drops vanilla extract

Whipped cream

Directions:

1. Remove the pistachio ice cream from its container and press it evenly into the bottom of a large metal bowl.
2. Remove the strawberry ice cream from its container and press it evenly on top of the layer of pistachio ice cream in the bowl.
3. Cover the bowl with plastic wrap and place it in the freezer until the ice cream is solid again.
4. Remove the vanilla ice cream from its container and place it in a large bowl; let the ice cream thaw a little.
5. Crush the walnuts and pistachios to a fine consistency.

6. Add the nuts, raisins, maraschino liqueur juice (or rum), vanilla extract, and whipped cream to the vanilla ice cream and stir well to combine.

7. Remove the bowl from the freezer and pour the vanilla ice cream mixture on top of the strawberry ice cream.

8. Cover the bowl again and place it back in the freezer until the vanilla ice cream is frozen.

9. When you are ready to serve the cassata, remove the bowl from the freezer and take the plastic wrap off.

10. Place the bowl upside down on a plate; hold the bowl tightly on the plate while briefly running warm water over the bowl.

11. Remove the plate and bowl from the water then carefully remove the bowl from the cassata.

12. Slice the cassata into quarters then serve.

Chapter 6: *Primo Piatto*
First Dish

I would occasionally apply at the most famous hotels around Frankfurt, but I never heard any responses. That didn't bother me too much, because there were so many beautiful restaurants. One such restaurant was The Börsenkeller, located near the Frankfurt stock exchange. "Börse" is a word related to the stock exchange, but it translates roughly to English as money purse, and of course "keller" is a cognate of cellar. The restaurant was a very busy place and the staff made good money, with wealthy and powerful diners from the nearby financial center coming to eat. The lure of making more money appealed to me.

I applied to the restaurant as a waiter and was hired two weeks later. I was settling into the restaurant's routine during my first week, when I was assigned a table of eight doctors. I was about to face a test. Like my train ride to Milan when I found the case stuffed with lire, I was about to find a large sum of money at my table.

After the doctors had left, I found a wallet on the floor under the table. One of them had lost it and had left, unaware. I picked it up and looked inside, checking for an ID. I could see the wallet contained a *lot* of deutschmarks.

It turned out that the wallet contained 1,215 marks, most of it in 100-mark bills—a little more than four hundred dollars at the time. That was a fortune, especially to me! For the briefest of moments, I was tempted to stuff the money into my pocket. I could keep my mouth shut (remaining silent in both Italian AND German) and just walk away.

But once again, my mama's words reached out to me quickly and squashed any such thoughts. I had made a vow to her that I would never steal again. Common sense also prevailed to slam the door on my temptation and banish the devil whispering to me.

No, I thought. I'm in Germany. If I got caught, I would be thrown in jail or forced to leave. I wouldn't take the risk. My path would take a decidedly wrong turn and my mama would have greatly disapproved. I would not disappoint her, or myself.

I walked toward the kitchen, where the manager was standing. "Here," I said, holding the wallet out to him, "I found this under one of my tables." A few minutes later, one of the doctors came running back into the restaurant.

Slightly out of breath, he asked the manager, "Have you found a wallet? I left my wallet behind." "Not to worry, sir. Yes, your waiter Carlo found it and turned it in." The man's relief was palpable. He thanked me, opened the wallet, and pulled out ten marks and handed it to me. I thanked him and tucked the money in my pocket. He departed, relieved to have his money and wallet safely back in his possession.

Later on, I brooded about how he'd nearly lost 1,215 marks and when he'd gotten it back, he had given me a measly ten marks. That was less than one percent. What a cheap guy. He gave me so little when he had so much. Honestly, I hadn't expected anything from the man, but it irritated me that it was so little. It was an insult. I would rather he just have left me with a hearty handshake and his gratitude.

I put the situation behind me and chose to focus on the new culinary opportunities that The Börsenkeller offered. The restaurant specialized not only in German food but also Italian and French. Much of what the chefs prepared in the kitchen made use of classical techniques that are the soul of the culinary education, which I still could not afford. However, I still had the trick up my sleeve from my days in Milan.

It wasn't long before I had a glass of wine in my hand and headed back into the kitchen. Presenting one of the chefs with the wine, he seemed happy to help as I asked him to teach me some new dish. Whether the kitchen was in Italy or Germany, it didn't matter. Wine was my admission form to enter the unofficial school of the professional chefs.

I especially recall getting the lowdown on two of our most popular dishes: veal chop with sauce Béarnaise and venison ragu with mushrooms. It was good, solid Central European cooking overall. These dishes were an elevated version of the foods long ago served in homes.

I got the feeling at that time that dishes such as these were served at fewer and fewer homes in any part of Europe. These traditional, home-cooked meals prepared by mothers or grandmothers were vanishing. The recipes, passed along by word of mouth and from mother to daughter, were in danger of being forgotten.

Before long, only professional chefs would preserve these priceless recipes. I filed away these recipes and cooking techniques as I watched the chefs in action. I knew I wanted to preserve these types of hearty, homestyle meals, and I planned for the day when I would open my own restaurant. I wanted to proudly serve my customers these traditional meals with simple, fresh ingredients.

With some money in my pocket now, I decided to treat myself to dinner for my birthday at a very popular restaurant in the city. It was almost nine o'clock and the restaurant was packed. Most of the diners were winding down their meal when the owner, Mario, would appear at the bar with a large bowl of fruit salad.

He would set the bowl on the bar top and ring a bell. "What liquor should I put in the fruit salad?" he would ask the guests. Then, Mario would turn around and gather various liquor bottles from the shelf. He would put up six or seven bottles on the counter, finishing up by grabbing a large gold-colored bottle of Coca-Cola.

The guests would variously scream, "No, no, no," or "Yes, yes, yes," about Mario's choices, until he silenced them with a shout of, "Who wants some fruit salad for dessert?" Right on cue, everybody would chant, "Me, me, me!"

I was so impressed by this little show that I introduced myself to Mario. We became friends, and I eventually asked him about the fruit salad. With a wink and a smile, he told me, "Carlo, that is just a show. Nothing goes inside the fruit salad except maraschino!" Maraschino is a smooth, sweet cherry liqueur. It was simply a way to get the customers engaged.

You never know where you will find inspiration. I learned a good trick, but it also gave me an idea for my own creation. I took this experience and decided to create my own recipe, based on his fruit salad.

Along with a very good selection of fruit and cherry liqueur, I added orange juice, lemon juice, and watermelon puree. I topped my concoction with a scoop of vanilla ice cream. That became the first recipe ever created by me, Carlo! It was a start for me on my path to become a chef. It was a simple dish, but it was my own creation. I was very proud of myself.

After about a year of working at the Börsenkeller, a co-worker mentioned that he had a friend who served food on a train. It was a long day, he said. His friend's shift began at five o'clock in the morning, when he would pitch in with the rest of the staff to stock supplies before the train departed Frankfurt. The train would stop in Bern, Switzerland, before reaching the Gare du Nord in Paris at two o'clock in the afternoon.

The train would return for Frankfurt from Paris in the early evening. The shift was around twenty hours long, but workers would get the next day off. They would have twenty-eight hours to themselves before the next shift. That was interesting, I thought.

Also, trains had always fascinated me, from those early days of eyeing the little station in Sanguinetto as I walked to school through my journeys to Milan and Frankfurt. Like my yellow bike and first car, they represented freedom, the ability to just leave where you were and go someplace different.

My co-worker said his friend made very good money. More money, trains, and new sights and scenery; it held a certain allure to me. I imagined going from Germany to Switzerland to France and back every other day, with some time to explore a little of Paris on each trip. And with some money in my pockets! I knew how much better I felt making a waiter's wages instead of a busboy's. It would be nice to make even more, save some, and really invest in my education.

My hunger emerged again, as well: I could not resist the idea of eating, and learning something about, that fabled French *cuisine classique*. I could possibly pick up some of the language, as well. This was an amazing opportunity to expand my skills and experience new countries. I was intrigued, so off I went to apply for the job. With my experience and language skills, I was soon employed as a waiter in the Frankfurt-Paris Rapide's dining car. I was twenty-three now, and ready for some changes.

In the dining car, the waitstaff all wore white gloves. I thought back to the Biffa, where I had first seen white-glove service. I was about to find out what it was like to serve while wearing gloves. On a moving train, no less. I was concerned about how to keep my gloves clean.

The actual food service was straightforward. Instead of bringing out large platters and serving individual dishes from a tray or cart beside the table, the staff brought each meal out on individual plates. We would pick up two or three plates from the kitchen through the compartment where the cooks placed them and head straight into the dining room. Each waiter had three tables and there were five or six waiters in the dining room. It was still elegant—or as elegant as we could manage on a jostling train, anyway.

The food was fairly simple, probably out of necessity considering the tight quarters in a train kitchen, called a galley like on a ship. It was a comfortable, happy mix of Italian and French, the European countries most well-known for their cuisines. Between meals, we waiters sold drinks, cigarettes, and chocolates.

On each leg of the journey (in those pre-European Union days), the staff would have to prepare for each country by having the local newspaper and currency ready—German deutschmarks, Swiss francs, and French francs.

When the train reached Paris in the afternoon, we had five hours to ourselves before we had to be back on the train that evening. It departed at seven o'clock, arriving back in Frankfurt's *bahnhof* at one o'clock in the morning.

In Paris, we headed off to explore different corners of the city. Of course, we all wanted to see the many famous landmarks such as the Eiffel Tower and the Arc de Triomphe and walk along the Champs-Élysées.

I was delighted to discover that learning French would not be nearly as difficult as learning German had been… I had spent nearly three years in Germany and had really struggled to learn the language. In just the few months I spent working on the train, I could speak better French than I could German. French and Italian were both so-called Romance languages, based on Latin, so words and syntax were similar enough.

We went to many different bistros during our layovers in Paris. We enjoyed the fact that the train stations, unlike airports, are usually in the middle of everything. We dined at many fine restaurants around the Gare du Nord until we found one particular place we really enjoyed, Chez Moi.

After discovering this restaurant, we returned time and time again. The chef, Bernard, recognized us as regulars and would come out and greet us with, "Hey, did you like my food?" I would reply, "*Oui, oui*, Bernard, *beaucoup*! Yes, very much."

One day, encouraged by his friendliness, I blurted out a question I'd been longing to ask: would he teach me some French cooking? I really enjoyed his escargot and many other dishes. I was astonished when he agreed. Impulsively, I kissed him on each cheek.

On return visits, he taught me how to make his escargot and duck a l'orange. It was a dream for me, learning French dishes and classic cooking techniques from a professional chef. Learning about French cuisine was a natural progression for me, after seeing Italian and German chefs in action.

French cuisine is said to have been heavily influenced by the Italians. Not only do the countries share a border, they share many similar types of recipes, meats, vegetables, herbs, cheeses, and beverages. In the mid-1500s, the Italian noblewoman Catherine dé Medici married Prince Henry of France, who later became King Henry II. Her father, as a wedding gift, sent personal chefs, vintners, produce gardeners, foodstuffs, grapes, drinks, and other resources.

French cuisine and cooking shifted in the seventeenth century as chefs worked hard to establish their own style and shift away from foreign influences. They took things to a whole new level, creating new sauces and techniques. They elevated and enhanced basic ingredients into elegant, refined dishes. They also wrote down their new recipes and shared them with the world for all time. They did this to a degree no Italian would have ever gotten around to doing, I think.

I admired this precision and these new approaches. Not only was I satisfying my lifelong hunger, I was absorbing all these new dishes and watching as Chef Bernard demonstrated his mastery of the craft. It was schooling I could never afford.

My time on this train line and its visits to Paris came to an end. I moved on to a new route, the Trans Europe Express connecting Zurich to Bern and Milan. The stop in Milan with this new job made me decide to return to Italy. After just over three months of working as a waiter on these trains traveling across three countries, I was ready to go home.

With my friends from Bologna and Seville, we made the return to our *patria*, our homeland. We felt that the addition of two languages, German and French, to our native tongue would allow us to find good, well-paying jobs at home. Our language abilities would help us find better jobs than most others working in restaurants in Italy.

Of course, my spirit was restless. You know I wasn't going to be satisfied with merely going back to work in an Italian restaurant. I had too much of the Italian explorers' blood of old in me. I had a yearning to continue my quest for knowledge.

Knowing German, French, and Italian at this point wasn't enough for me. Earning money wasn't my primary motivation. What I wanted was to keep on learning. And that meant a new language, of course. This time, I decided English was my next language to learn. English, after all, was spoken all over the world. I wanted to be able to speak it too.

I insisted to my friends that we take the next big step: to England. We wasted no time in seeking out the employment agent I had previously used in Milan. In February 1966, we applied for jobs in England. A few weeks after that, The Kettner Restaurant in London called to offer employment.

Soon, our visas were in place, along with all the other documents for admittance into the country and employment at Kettner's. We loaded into my trusty Opal and headed out from Milan in the direction on London. We crossed through a part of Switzerland and a lot of France before arriving at the car ferry that left Calais for Dover, the port with the famous white cliffs.

It was an easy process to cross the English Channel from France to England. We drove the car onto the ferry and within a short time, we were headed across the Channel. The boat trip took a little over two hours and we were back on solid ground shortly before noon.

"Carlo, don't forget," my friend Roberto said, turning to me as I maneuvered us away from the docks. "They drive on the wrong side of the road." I looked at him, puzzled. "What do you mean?" "They drive on the left side, not on the right side, like we do." We drove off the boat, in a line of cars, so I just followed the cars in front of me.

But I soon saw what Roberto had meant. Oncoming traffic was now on our right, instead of our left. It was confusing, to say the least. I could manage all right when there was plenty of traffic, so I could just follow a car heading in our direction. I was quite glad I had my own car and was not driving an English car, where the steering wheel is on the right. That would have added to my confusion.

When there were no cars around me, it was easiest to forget. I would drift to the right without thinking, and suddenly see oncoming traffic coming toward me. All I could do was quickly jerk the wheel to the left. The worst was driving on roundabouts (what the British call traffic circles, usually with streets spooling off them in different directions).

It was too tempting, without much traffic, to curve to the right on these traffic circles, which are one way. At first, it was scary and gave me a few headaches. Ultimately though, it was like learning to speak a new language with new rules. This was the story of my life, right? I learned fast after a couple of days on the roads. I'm glad I adjusted so quickly—I didn't need to be involved in another accident!

When we arrived at the restaurant, we gave the host who greeted us a bit of a short-lived thrill, since he assumed our entire party was arriving for dinner. I remembered the bellboy at the hotel in Germany when he grabbed my case thinking I was a guest.

We disappointed the host, though. No, we weren't here to eat—only for work. The host took the news in good spirits, though, unlike the bellboy who immediately dropped my case. The host passed us on to the manager. The manager had a smile for each of us, then provided dinner in the employee cafeteria as he explained the rules of the house.

He told us we needed to be ready to work at nine o'clock the next morning. I was back to being a busboy until I learned enough English to apply for a waiter position. The manager took us on a tour of the place and explained its interesting history.

The Kettner was located in the Soho section of London and opened in 1867. It was one of the first French restaurants in London, owned by the former chef for Napoleon Bonaparte, Auguste Kettner. The prince of Wales, later to become the future King Edward VII, was rumored to have courted his mistress, the British-American actress Lillie Langtry, at the Kettner. The authors Oscar Wilde and Agatha Christie were regulars at the restaurant, as were many other celebrities over its almost century-long history.

The Kettner was a very elegant restaurant, famous for high-class clientele from all over the world. The food and service here matched the best I had seen in Italy. When the wife of the Shah of Iran walks in, you know you're working in someplace special. The same went for many ministers from foreign governments and an endless sprinkling of posh British MPs, or Members of Parliament.

Although I worked in such a marvelous place, I was back to being a busboy. A busboy who had to scrimp and save. During my first few weeks living in London, I didn't drive much. First and foremost, I couldn't afford to fill the tank with what the English called petrol.

Also, I didn't speak or understand enough English yet. I didn't know many words, although I knew three important ones very well: please, thank you, and hello. It's hard to navigate if you can't read the street signs. That was one of the first things I learned to translate in Germany.

Fortunately, my apartment was close to the restaurant. It was usually best for me to walk to work. Back to hoofing it. Oh well, I was used to it. I had walked countless miles in my life, so what were a few more at this point?

At the end of my first week, I went to a bank to open an account. I wanted to deposit all the money I had saved while working in Germany, around three thousand two hundred marks, (about eight hundred dollars back then). The English equivalent would have been nearly three hundred pounds.

I presented all the money I had in the world to the teller and struggled to communicate my desire. Instead of opening an account for me, a bank staff member called the police! When they arrived, they asked me all sorts of questions. Naturally I couldn't understand them. Finally, I figured out that they wanted to know where I had gotten the deutschmarks, thinking perhaps I had stolen them.

I had faced challenges in the past, finding large sums of money. I had never taken any money in my life (my worst crime was stealing fruit and other food to eat). Now that I had some money of my own, earned through hard work, I was accused of stealing. I couldn't believe it.

Those words came back to me: respect and discipline. I knew they would get me through this. "Me got bankbook," I said, stumbling over my words. "What do you mean? You have a bankbook? Where?" the officer asked. "In my wagen." (German for car.) "Show me," the officer demanded.

He followed me to my car, where I retrieved my bankbook. I showed the officer, as the book listed my withdrawal and closure of my German bank account. I went back inside and showed it to the tellers, who apologized profusely. "Please, Mr. Molinaro, we are so sorry. Sit down."

I didn't have time now, so I explained in my limited English, "I have to go back to work. I am late now. I will come back tomorrow." Something came up and I didn't get a chance to go back to the bank the next day. Instead, over lunch at the cafeteria, I told some of my co-workers what had happened. "I went to deposit all my money in the bank and they wouldn't take it. So now I have to go back and try to deposit it again."

Well, that was a mistake. Two days later, I looked under the mattress where I'd tucked all my money. It was gone. I couldn't believe it. I was devastated. The thoughts swirled through my head: the money I had worked so hard for, all the pleasantries of life I had gone without, my plans for attending a formal cooking school. I felt sick.

What had happened to it? I ran through different scenarios in my head until I recalled telling my co-workers about it during lunch in the cafeteria. One of those co-workers rented the room next to mine. The next day I went to work, primed to confront him. My worst fears came true. The guy did not show up for his shift.

"How come he's not here today?" I asked someone, feeling frantic and anxious. They didn't know. After my shift, I went and knocked on his door. Nobody answered. A neighbor heard me knocking and came out. "He's gone," he said. "Gone where?" I fired back. "I don't know, but he left," came the reply.

I told the landlord what had happened, but there was nothing he could do. The guy was gone. And so were all of my hard-earned deutschmarks, everything I had. I considered calling the police, but I figured it would do no good. I was sure he was long gone. The money I had been accused of stealing—which prevented me from depositing it—had been stolen.

I felt ill, sad, and betrayed that I had trusted this guy as my friend. He had come into my room and taken all I had, nearly two years' salary. It was a bitter lesson to learn.

My mama had never warned me about such things, as we never had any money to worry about.

Another obstacle to block my path, a challenge to overcome. I wistfully thought about how much I had earned working on the train. I would just have to start over. Still, at least I was making seven pounds a week as a busboy instead of the paltry less than one pound a week I'd earned in Germany doing the same work.

I channeled my frustration and anger, focusing on working hard. I learned about the food and, most of all, the language. One week salary out of each month paid the rent. The other three weeks, my money went for food and whatever else I needed. I saved whatever I could, but it would be a long time before I had built up to what I had lost.

I always set a little aside to go to the movies or buy books and magazines so I could study the language. Within two months, I had a good understanding of English and was promoted to waiter. Now, I could speak and understand four different languages. Immersion in a culture is a great way to learn a new language. Pick up the lingo or struggle mightily.

At the Kettner, waiters picked up the customers' food on individual plates, like we did on the train, and brought them to the diners. We didn't take the orders, though. The maître d', referred to as the captain, greeted the customers and took their orders. We also didn't handle any side-table preparations like I had at some restaurants, where we would do tasks like cutting meat or deboning fish.

After working at the restaurant for a while, I pulled out the same trick that I successfully used before. I made friends with the chef. The chef was from Rhodesia (now called Zimbabwe) but had French training. He also spoke a little French, as did I after exploring Paris and taking care of many French passengers on the train.

I would ask some questions about some special dishes like roast beef or the famous British special dish "kidney pie," but I was not impressed. English cuisine was vastly different from French or Italian. Along with kidney and other meat pies, popular dishes included stews, grilled or fried foods, and boiled vegetables. Simple and fresh could not be used to describe many of the dishes.

The week before I was promoted to waiter, I had saved enough money again to enroll in language classes. I selected the Berlitz School of English; it was not very expensive and the classes were basic. It was within walking distance of the restaurant, so I saved money by not having to drive. I attended classes for two hours in the afternoon, twice a week.

The courses taught me the alphabet, pronunciation, and things like that. It was a slow process because, like German, English wasn't that similar to Italian. English proved easier to learn than German, though, and the classes really helped me. Trying to learn on your own is so vastly different than being taught by a good teacher in a supportive environment.

Deep down, it simply felt good to be in a classroom learning something of immense value to me. I was a model student and worked diligently to learn. I was very motivated, as well.

When I was living outside of Italy, I watched people closely. It is not just about learning the language. You must also learn and respect the culture. This is what my mother meant about respect. When you go someplace new, you must respect their traditions and their way of doing things.

I understood early on to become a student of culture. Study the people, watch their habits and mannerisms. See how they interact with each other. Work to blend in and integrate with them, rather than stubbornly insisting on doing things the way they are done back home.

In London, everyone wore a coat and carried an umbrella. You never went anywhere without an umbrella. When you go out in the morning, it is sunny. You think *why did I bring a coat?* A few hours later, the wind begins to blow and you are glad to have a coat. Then the rain comes. The English are prepared for that by having their umbrella, or brolly. So to fit in, and for practical reasons as well, I always had my coat and umbrella, no matter what.

Even though I was highly trained as a waiter by this point, I worked diligently to learn more. After working at the Kettner for six months, I decided I needed to spend some time improving my kitchen skills. I became the director of outside catering for a fellow Italian, named Franco Grimelli, at Trattoria Roma. Though the business was named for Rome, both Grimelli and his chef hailed from Florence in Tuscany.

Italian cooking is very regional, so working here introduced me to yet another great group of dishes and food traditions. Florence had long been considered a culinary haven for many decades in my home country. The dishes and cooking styles were connected to the Florentines from the Renaissance period; in some cases, they went all the way back to the Etruscans living in the area before the Roman Empire.

This was the next big step along my journey. Finally, I was officially involved in preparing food. For so many years, I had served as a busboy or waiter working in the front of the house. Now, I would join the kitchen staff. It had been a long, difficult road to get here, and I was extremely excited.

My time in London was remarkable, but I must admit I saw, heard, and experienced very little of the city itself and its electric environment. This was the mid-1960s and a revolution of new music and sweeping cultural changes were everywhere. Bands like The Beatles, The Rolling Stones, and many other groups were launching the British Invasion that would sweep the U.S. and other countries. This was also the time of Twiggy, one of the hottest models of the day, and all the mod fashions found along Carnaby Street.

Any of these people might have dined in one of the restaurants I worked in, but I probably would not have realized it. Frankly, I suspected the places were too old-fashioned for their taste. The restaurants just weren't cool or hip, in the slang of the day. Nightclubs and discos were more likely their scene.

Dancing, partying, and drinking were one of the many things I simply had no time to do. No money and no interest. A new country, a new language, and a weekly paycheck were about the only things that interested me. Had I been working in Rome during the Empire or in Paris during the Revolution, I'm sure I would have missed out on those, too!

I did sample some English dishes, such as kidney pie and fish and chips. My opinion? No thank you. Why was everything wrapped in dough or fried? The best food I had in England was Italian, especially this pizza place I found in Trafalgar Square. Of course, it was run by two Italians who had left their homeland like I had.

One day I met an Italian customer named Sergio Pellegrini. It was nice to speak with a fellow countryman. We got to talking about the restaurant business and he expressed surprise when I told him I was making seven pounds a week. "Seriously? You can make that in a day where I live, in Bermuda." "I don't believe you," I said, incredulous to his claim. "No, no, it's true," he assured me. Well, that was all I needed to hear.

I was curious now. "What would I need to emigrate? Do you know?" I asked. He laughed. "All you need is to come with a return ticket. Buy a two-way ticket, not one-way, and have your passport. That is all you need." Okay, I wondered, "Why a two-way ticket?" He replied "Because you cannot stay indefinitely. That's against the law there. But you can come for a few years."

He scribbled a few words on a piece of paper and handed it to me. How many times in my life had a few words scribbled on a piece of paper pointed me towards my next chapter? He had provided his address. "Write to me if you want to come to

Bermuda. I will get you a job there. You will love it." He smiled warmly. "You won't need a coat or an umbrella. Well, maybe bring your umbrella," he said with a chuckle. My next destination was now marked on my map.

I wrote to the hotel, but when I didn't hear anything for some time, I figured Sergio was just bragging. Maybe there was no such hotel or a well-paying job. Instead, I worked at Trattoria Roma. It wasn't a very luxurious restaurant, but it was good for me. I could practice my English and speak with the customers while working side-by-side with the chef in the kitchen.

Let me digress a little. Before I started at Trattoria Roma, I had a three-week waiting period. I veered from my path for that brief period of time, deciding to live a little. I had been working for much of my life. Like mythic explorers, I had succumbed to a siren call from the female of our species.

I met a girl from Spain at a café along Oxford Street in the West End of London, famous for its shopping. Until this point, I never made the time or had the money to date anyone seriously. So, after meeting this girl I decided to do something I had never done in my life. I scheduled my first ever vacation. Yes, I parted with my money in the name of love and went to visit her in Spain.

My special recipe for you: Chef Carlo's Ensalata di Fruta

A simple fruit salad is a marvelous dish, well suited for almost any occasion. The trick is to use the freshest possible fruits, so you can vary the types used by their seasonal availability.

I created my version of a fruit salad after being inspired by the show put on by the owner of one of the more popular restaurants in Frankfurt.

This was my first effort to create a dish that was truly mine. It's nothing fancy, but simple and fresh is what makes this dish still appealing after all these years.

Serving size: 4

Ingredients:

1 medium-size apple

1 peach

1 pear

1 orange

1 mango

1 small watermelon

1 cup strawberries

1 cup pineapple

Sauce

    Juice of 2 medium oranges

    Juice of 1 lemon

    2 tablespoons sugar

    4 tablespoons maraschino liqueur

    2 tablespoons watermelon puree (or 1 tablespoon melted vanilla ice cream)

Directions:

1. Wash all the fruit thoroughly and dry it off.
2. Dice the fruit into small pieces, about a quarter of an inch in size.
3. Place all the fruit into a serving bowl.
4. In a small bowl, add the orange juice, lemon juice, sugar, maraschino liqueur, and watermelon puree (or ice cream); combine until all ingredients are mixed well.

5. Pour the sauce over the fruit and toss until well blended.

6. You can place the fruit salad in the refrigerator until chilled or serve it right away. You can add a scoop of high-quality vanilla ice cream to each serving, if desired.

Chapter 7: *L'amore è Nell'Aria*

Love is in the Air

In June, 1966, I packed some clothes and got into my Opal. I was on my way to Spain. The girl I was planning to visit told me she was working for Iberia Airlines in Barcelona as an administration officer. We had met in the café, discussing how she had just finished taking a course in English, as I had done. The conversation continued from there, and next thing you know, I was planning a trip to see her.

My plan was to reverse my original course from when I first arrived in England. I would cross the English Channel, taking the ferry back to France. I would drive southeast through France, head over the border into Spain, and continue to Barcelona on the Mediterranean Coast. It would take me over fifteen hours to make the trip, including the ferry.

I left in the morning, getting out of London and on the ferry as early as possible. Before long, I was in France and ready to continue my long drive. Along the way, I saw a French soldier looking for a ride. I stopped to pick him up. The soldier climbed in and said he was heading to a location near Paris.

I asked him if we were heading in the correct direction towards Brie, France. Brie, known for its famous cheese, was a landmark I was using on the way to Barcelona; it was roughly my halfway point. He assured me I was. He was a soldier, so I trusted him.

We made it to where he was going; I dropped him off and continued on my trek. Shortly, I realized I was heading in the wrong direction. The soldier had told me I was going the right way so I would give him a ride, even though it was out of my way. I stopped and asked a policeman for directions. He helped get me pointed in the correct direction. I thanked him, deciding I wouldn't be giving anybody else a ride.

As I approached Brie in the early afternoon that day, I was driving around a sharp curve up a hill. In the opposite direction, a driver was coming straight towards me. To avoid a head-on collision, I swerved to the right. My car hit the rail, flipping over and rolling down the hill. My world went topsy-turvy and the car landed upside down.

Dazed, I was able to crawl out of the car. I checked myself over; through God's grace, I hadn't suffered even a scratch. I was thankful that I was driving my tough Opal and not a little car, like my Fiat. Shortly, the police arrived and filled out a report. The other driver had fled the scene. The accident caused so much damage to my car that it was written off as a total loss.

Two cars, two accidents, two totals. Unfortunately, there would be many more such days. I seem to be a magnet for accidents. Only one would be my fault, but the end result is the same. One of my most profound talents must be being in the wrong place at the wrong time.

That was it for my travels that day. I got a hotel room in Brie. After getting some sleep, I woke up and took a train to Barcelona the next day. That was fine with me. Trains had always safely delivered me to my destination.

As soon as I arrived in Barcelona, I called my new girlfriend and told her what had happened to me. She immediately came to the train station, concerned about my welfare. I assured her I was fine, and we set out from the station to enjoy Barcelona and the surrounding area.

My vacation in Barcelona was amazing. We enjoyed all the happiness that young love can. We visited many places in the city and nearby sites, including the famous artsy beach community called Sitges. We took in a bullfight; Spain's famous blood sport was extremely popular at the time. We also went to see the most beautiful, authentic flamenco dance on Montjuic, a hill overlooking the city.

Taking in Barcelona with my girlfriend was such a marvelous experience. I really relaxed and enjoyed it. My first real vacation was going beyond my expectations. Unfortunately, the time passed too quickly as it does when you're lost in love and soaking up all the sights, sounds, and tastes of new culture.

On our final day together, we dined at the Rivoli Restaurant overlooking architect Antonio Gaudi's magnificent fountain. The food, company, and view were exquisite. The evening ended, and it was time for me to leave the next day. We parted ways, thinking that we would be together soon, as love always makes us think.

Before I left, I considered staying with her and finding a job in Barcelona. However, it was difficult for foreigners to obtain work in Spain. Generalissimo Francisco Franco, the country's military dictator, had imposed strict self-sufficiency policies that restricted work opportunities for non-natives. Franco had been in power since his side won the Spanish Civil War, prior to the start of World War II.

It proved impossible for me to find a job; I tried many times. Barcelona was under Franco's thumb more than any other part of Spain. It had been his enemy's headquarters during the civil war. The dictator never tired of punishing the people of the area for what their parents and grandparents had done.

He waged a cultural war against the millions of people in the region, suppressing their arts and literature while outlawing their language, Catalan. He impressed on the independence-mind people the need for a unified cultural and economic alignment under a single Spanish government.

The bottom line for me? My dream of moving to Spain slowly faded away. I never got a job there where I could stay with my girlfriend. I returned to England and stayed. My once-strong commitment to my girlfriend to return, as well as my feelings for her, faded.

This broke my heart a little each step of the way. Letters between me in London and to her, via her parents' home off the elegant Paseo de Gracia, became fewer and farther between. Eventually neither of us felt like we loved each other. Only the cherished memories of my time with her remained as the relationship faded.

Dejected, I decided I needed a change. I wrote another letter to the hotel on the island of Bermuda that Sergio Pellegrini had told me about during my time at the Kettner. Once again, I waited for a response. In the meantime, I continued to work at Trattoria Roma.

I didn't realize at the time how much working at the restaurant would change my life forever. My non-existent love life was about to improve, even as I was nursing the hurt I'd carried home from Spain. I was about to meet another lady.

There was a frequent customer to the restaurant who I noticed. She was attractive and dressed nicely. One day, I struck up a conversation with her. Her name was Sofia, and she was nice, very intelligent, and well mannered. I immediately told her she was a very pretty lady, feeling bold after my initial adventures in the land of love to the sunny south. I offered to take her out for a coffee later and she accepted.

Sofia was Portuguese but had not spent much time at all in her native country. She had, in fact, been born in the Portuguese colony of Macao in China. Her father practiced medicine there, before returning to Portugal in the late-1940s. Later, he got a job with the Health Department at the port of Luanda in Angola and moved his family with him. She spent most of her childhood living in Portuguese Africa.

As we spoke about her life, I felt my geographic horizons broadening and shifting once again. I told Sofia I was studying English at the Berlitz School. She replied that she planned to enroll there too. She began taking classes there, which was good for me. We saw each other quite often. The following January, in 1967, we both switched to a new school called Queensway and studied English for the entire year. Sofia and I became very close friends.

In late November/early December, I finally heard from the hotel in Bermuda that I had written to. I received an application for employment at The Princess Hotel. The famous hotel and resort first opened its doors in 1885. It was named in honor of Princess Louise, Queen Victoria's fourth daughter. She had visited Bermuda two years prior to the hotel opening and referred to the island as a "place of eternal spring." Sounds like I could ditch the coat, but still bring the umbrella.

Dubbed "The Pink Palace" by locals in Bermuda, many wealthy people and famous celebrities have stayed at the hotel during its storied history. Mark Twain would smoke cigars on the veranda and amuse other guests; Ian Fleming, creator of James Bond, was inspired by the hotel's fish tank-lined gazebo bar and it became an element in his *Dr. No* novel.

The hotel only hires once a year, in the spring. The resort business is very seasonal, especially in those days. I had practically finished my English course when I got the application. I felt confident I could handle working as a waiter in an English-speaking country.

As a sign of our deepening relationship, I talked to Sofia about what I should do. I wanted to hear her thoughts on me applying for a position there. She was very understanding—sad, but understanding. It was a terrific career opportunity, she assured me, and I could not afford to pass it up.

With Sofia's encouragement, I submitted my application for a waiter position. I was hired and began to make plans for my big journey. I was going to leave Europe AND travel by air for the first time in my life, venturing to the oh-so-British island in the Atlantic Ocean. I was anxious but enthusiastic.

Our English class ended before Christmas. Shortly after the New Year, I packed up, got my paperwork in order, and bought my round-trip airline ticket to the island. Sofia and I said our bittersweet goodbyes. For my part, I promised her I would return to London and visit as soon as possible.

The Princess was a premier luxury property and the service was said to be impeccable. I had learned a lot about the restaurant trade in Italy, Germany, France, and England, but I knew I could learn so much more working at such a classy establishment in Bermuda. The prospect was incredibly exciting.

I settled in my new place, the hotel dormitory. I was fortunate to be assigned as a waiter in the gourmet dining restaurant, the Tiara Room, not the standard dining room. Every dish came out on a silver tray for delivery to the guests. I had not experienced this kind of service for a long time, since I worked at Savini and the Cavalieri Hotel in Milan.

I was assigned to assist the captain, responsible for taking food from the kitchen to the diners. I also helped prepare certain dishes tableside. I would bring the food out for the tableside preparation and watch carefully as the captain prepared it. As I became familiar with the dishes, I began handing him the necessary ingredients before he asked for them. I felt a little bit like an experienced nurse assisting the surgeon in an operating room, if you'll allow me that comparison.

The work was exhausting. It was worth the hard work though, despite the exhaustion I felt at the end of my shift. For me, it was another opportunity to add to my growing knowledge of the restaurant business.

The time I spent in the kitchen introduced me to one of the most professional chefs I'd worked with so far. His name was Andy, and he was from France. He reminded me a little of Chef Bernard at that little bistro in Paris. "If you like cooking," he said, "watch me and you will learn, for sure."

Since I was in the kitchen quite often, I would always ask him questions. Sometimes, Chef Andy would run me out of the kitchen, especially when hundreds of meals had to be hustled out quickly to our guests. But I never gave up. Bit by bit, I learned a lot of new recipes and some great techniques from my chef friend in the kitchen.

I would practice everything I learned whenever I could. Before long, my dreams of opening my own place someday had flourished. Now, I was twenty-seven and had over a decade of experience in the restaurant business. Starting as a busboy in Milan, I had become a waiter and took every opportunity to talk with chefs and learn new dishes and techniques. Why pay for cooking school? I was gaining invaluable first-hand experience from some of the best chefs in high-class restaurants.

Now, I could communicate in English, German, French, and Italian, of course. I had worked in Italy, Germany, England, and Bermuda, plus France and Switzerland if you count my experience on the train. Through all that, the two words that I lived by were respect and discipline. They had served me well this far.

Respect and discipline were key at the Princess. Wealthy, famous, and powerful guests were always staying at the hotel. You had to maintain your professionalism no matter who the guest was—you couldn't get star-struck. Among our regular customers at the Princess were tennis champion Bjorn Borg and movie star Dustin Hoffman. You certainly couldn't ask for autographs or photos. Just provide impeccable service.

Hoffman used to hang out with my best friend Rudi Paul, who also worked at the Princess. Paul was born behind the Iron Curtain in East Germany before escaping to the West; he eventually moved to America and opened his own restaurant in Baltimore. He had been in the restaurant business about the same length of time I had, starting as a teenager like me.

Bermuda is a British territory, so not only would we would see movie stars and celebrities, but members of the Royal Family as well. Prince Charles, the Prince of Wales and father to Prince Harry and William, came to Bermuda in 1970. The Prince was there to open the 350th session of Parliament at the Government House.

The Princess Hotel handled the catering for the event, and I was working at one of the cocktail parties. The Prince seemed very nice and down to earth, I thought. I was passing by the guests, offering hors d' oeuvres. Someone accidentally bumped into me as I was near the Prince.

To my horror, several canapés fell to the floor. As I bent to pick them up, I was astonished when Prince Charles leaned over and helped me. This was the Prince of Wales. And he was helping a waiter pick up spilled food. I apologized profusely, of course, but he brushed it aside with a kind smile. It was no big deal to him.

We not only served famous people, we also served a dish that was famous, in its own way. These days, the dish is very well known and numerous restaurants serve it (although most pale in comparison to the original). At one time, Hollywood celebrities considered this dish all the rage and filled the tables at the few restaurants that served it. This dish was originated in the 1920s by an Italian American and it bears his name: the Caesar Salad, created by Caesar Cardini.

Cardini was from a big Italian family, like me. He immigrated to America and operated restaurants in San Diego and Mexico. He reportedly invented the salad when a rush of holiday diners caused his restaurant to run low on supplies. He made due with what he had in the kitchen, and thus arose this new type of salad. He even prepared the salad for a young Julia Child and her parents at tableside (the way it was originally served). Child would later include the original recipe in one of her cookbooks.

One of our dining room captains, a Spaniard named Antonio Perez, went to Mexico on vacation. Two big outcomes from the trip were: 1) he married a lovely young Mexican woman, and 2) he met Caesar Cardini in Tijuana.

Cardini was a legend in our industry by this point, and Antonio convinced Caesar to teach him how to make the salad exactly the way Cardini always had. When Antonio got back to Bermuda, he taught us the recipe. It's the recipe I would follow, tableside or in the kitchen, for the rest of my career.

Talent abounded at the Princess. A few of the waiters could sing or play the piano. One waiter was a painter; the hotel hung one of his paintings in the lobby. He sold a number of his works to hotel guests, many of whom came to admire and collect his work.

A number of restaurant staffers were talented soccer players. There were enough of them to field a team for the Princess, and they were good enough to play some matches against Bermuda's national team. One time they even beat them, and the hotel proudly displayed the trophy in the lobby.

My focus had always been developing my cooking talents and language skills. My once melodious voice soured due to some health problems, and I couldn't sing like when I used to serenade the girls in Cerea. I wasn't as very good at soccer, either. It's hard to learn to play if you don't even have a ball growing up.

I did make some time to enjoy my life in paradise at our seaside resort, though. My girlfriend Sofia was living so far away. So, rather than be lonely in my free time, I decided to learn how to swim and play tennis. Growing up, we didn't see the ocean. The water in Bermuda was so amazing and blue. This was heaven to me. Sometimes I enjoyed just sitting in the sand and gazing out at the water. I was having the time of my life, or as much as could without my Sofia.

The local cuisine was a little more intriguing to me than some of my other culinary experiences in my previous stops around Europe. There were a lot of seafood dishes I tried. I wasn't too keen on the seasonings, though. And since the island was influenced by the British, some of the cuisine was influenced by the English cooking style.

Despite living in such an amazing location with such wonderful scenery, our social opportunities were limited. Most of the hotel staff was male; there were very few females and we weren't permitted to socialize with the guests. But that didn't stop some of the staff from trying.

Only the dining room captains were allowed to speak directly to the guests. This severely hampered some of the male staff's desire to "chat up" female guests of, shall we say, undetermined marital status. This didn't deter some of the more brazen staff members, though. They found a way around this rule. Their sneaky solution? Placing written notes in the menus that were presented to certain ladies.

These notes would read, "Would you like to go out tonight?" and suggest times and places to meet, like later at the discotheque. The men participating in this proposed extracurricular activity would show up at the rendezvous point and hope the for the best.

However, one of these messages mistakenly ended up in the menu of an older lady, who was incensed. In a huff, she immediately reported the errant note to the maître d'. He spoke to the manager, who quickly called a meeting. The manager admonished us all, stating, "The next time you pull a stunt like that, you will be fired. No excuses. No exceptions." That put an abrupt halt to the note passing.

Those are just some of my many recollections of working at the Princess. However, some of my most important memories, and a vital takeaway in my restaurant experience, was what didn't happen—the continual and almost universal war between front of the house and back.

I have worked at many restaurants and understand how the work environment can become extremely high pressure. I have seen first-hand the animosity that can exist between the front of the house staff and kitchen staff. In some restaurants, the conflict starts out as nothing more than a blame game. The waiters and managers blame the kitchen staff for messing up the food, and the kitchen staff blames the waiters and managers for botching the service.

The situation boils over and the two sides entrench against the other. Each believes his side to be utterly blameless, especially when there is even the slightest customer complaint. Things can quickly get out of hand. Soon it escalates into an all-out war (I use this word instead of rivalry or argument). There is much screaming and yelling, sometimes pushing, shoving, and punching.

Every so often a knife or sauté pan is delivered to some part of the body. In such cases, besides getting medical attention for an injured worker, the best a manager can do is try to keep the conflict contained to the kitchen and the volume down so no paying customer is disturbed.

That's the way things usually are between the front and the back. I experienced this more intensely and personally in my career because I was determined to master the jobs of both. I could see the point of view of both sides. I understood the mindset and attitudes of busboy and waiters, while striving to enter the world of professional chefs and cooks.

At the Princess, however, this rivalry never developed. I don't know why this was for sure. A big part of it was probably better management. Better pay for the staff may have contributed, also. Certainly the chance to live and work in such an idyllic, tranquil part of the world helped as well. It's hard to get worked up about much in such a serene, peaceful setting.

The environment fostered a team approach between front and back of the house. There was a real camaraderie. I'm not saying we were merely encouraged to be a team or forced to be one; we truly were. Occasionally, the Princess would throw a staff party at a house owned by the hotel across the bay. Everyone would attend, from the chambermaids and front desk people to all the food and beverage employees, including the maître d'. It was good that we all got along so well because Bermuda is a very small island with only twenty thousand people.

As proof of this team-first attitude and the how well we got along, some of my closest, lifelong friendships grew out of the Princess team. Every year or two, there's a Princess reunion somewhere and we all try to attend. There's a lot more white hair in our crowd now, a lot more talk of medical procedures upcoming or just completed. But we all feel committed to each other. With the proliferation of technology, email, and social media, we all stay more in touch now than ever before.

Somebody at the Princess did something right a long time ago. Once again, I can't put my finger on what exactly went into creating and fostering that team spirit, but it happened. It was the perfect blend of the right staff, the right management, and the right environment.

The proof that the hotel brought in the right staff is demonstrated by the success so many of us found in life and business after leaving for other challenges. Many of us, whether front or back of the house, ended up opening restaurants in cities across America. I would eventually settle in Houston, Texas, and run my own restaurant for over twenty-eight years.

A few staff members from Italy made their way back to their native land, as all of us Italians have talked about doing someday once we had made some money. They opened their own restaurants once back there.

One of the greatest success stories was our own Princess pastry chef, Roland Mesnier. After he left he moved up to a new address and a quite famous one: 1600 Pennsylvania Avenue. He began a multi-decade run in that job for the President of the United States; his creations were enjoyed by multiple presidents and visitors to the White House between 1975 and 2004.

One of my fondest memories, and lessons that stuck with me, is Chef Roland telling me that true French crepes have to be thin enough you can read a newspaper through them. He also shared his recipes, and experiences at the White House, with the world, authoring several books.

Several months after I moved to Bermuda, I met an English family who were guests of the hotel. We became very friendly. I told them that I'd lived and worked in London before coming to Bermuda. I explained how much I liked being in that great city and learning English.

As a gift, they gave me an expensive gold lighter that someone had given them. "We don't smoke," they said, explaining someone had given it to them. I didn't smoke either, but I knew someone who did—Sofia.

So I accepted the gift and expressed my appreciation. I packaged the lighter up for Sofia and enclosed a note. "This is for you," I jotted. She wrote back, "I am enjoying it very much, thank you." She asked "When are you coming to London for a visit?" I replied that she should take some time and come visit me in sun-drenched Bermuda, away from foggy, rainy London.

I had stumbled upon a house, fully furnished, that was available for rent. It belonged to a wealthy doctor and his wife who lived in Canada, and amazingly, I could afford the monthly rental. I let Sofia know I had a place for her to stay.

Sofia finished school the following September and came to visit me. It was the best birthday I could remember. I was thrilled to have her there. I kept telling her, "You have finished school now, so you don't have to go back."

We were enjoying our time together on the island. It did not take much to convince her to stay. Not only did she stay, she agreed to marry me. Five months later, on February 20, 1969 we married. The ceremony took place in Hamilton, Bermuda. We, the happy couple, arrived at the church in a horse-drawn carriage with about twenty of my Princess co-workers following us on Vespas. Quite the procession.

My mama would be so excited that I now was married, had a good job that paid well, and was living in paradise. I'm sure my family back home in Italy would not believe what I had achieved. I had journeyed from poverty and hunger in a small village in Italy, being forced to leave school after second grade, to working throughout Europe, learning several new languages, and building my skills in the restaurant industry.

After the ceremony, the wedding party returned to my house. We enjoyed finger foods and wine through the night. The next day, we were all back at work. But Sofia and I were soon jetting off on our honeymoon. The trip was the farthest I'd ever traveled by air. We flew from Bermuda to London, on to Lisbon, and then on to the colony of Angola in West Africa.

Her parents still lived in Angola, so we were heading to visit them there; I would meet them for the first time. Between that and getting married, it was an exciting and very emotional time. My Portuguese wasn't very good, but her parents understood Italian well enough. We are able to communicate, more or less. They were very well-educated people.

Her mother spoke some English and her father a little less so. That's one of the reasons they sent their daughter to England, as they wanted her to learn English. Of course, that worked out for me since this led to our meeting and provided a mutual topic for our early talks.

I enjoyed the trip and our stay in Angola very much. However, a newlywed couple needs some time alone, so Sofia and I took leave of her parents. We decided to take a road trip to see more of the country, so we rented a Jeep and took off. We planned to travel from the capital city of Luanda on the coast to East Nova Lisboa (now called Huambo) in the central western region of the country.

We would then drive toward the neighboring countries of northern Rhodesia (now Zambia) then south to near the border of Namibia. We would head back into Angola from there, stopping at a lovely seaport on the Atlantic Ocean, Lobito. We would then head north up the coast back to Luanda.

I was a little nervous when I got behind the wheel. I thought of my first trip to England and how I had to adjust to driving on the left. I didn't want to repeat my early lapses where I would drift into the other lane and see an oncoming car.

"Wait," I said to my new wife, "which side of the road do they drive on here, right or left?" "In Africa," she laughed, "they drive in the middle." I glanced over at her, alarmed, but she was joking. Well, half-joking.

We took our time, soaking in the diversity of the habitats and taking opportunities to view many different types of wild animals. I couldn't believe my eyes.

This wasn't Italy! There were so many new and wondrous sights for me to behold. What made this time even more special was sharing it with Sofia, my bride.

Our time in Africa was winding down, and we were heading towards the Angolan coast and Lobito. That's when my bad luck with vehicles caught up to me. I thought I had left it behind in Europe, but no luck.

We had a mishap a couple of hours before reaching Lobito. I took a curve, lost control, and the Jeep flipped over. Remarkably, neither of us was hurt. We were just shaken up. At that point, it was seven o'clock at night and we didn't know where to go. We had no idea how many more miles lay ahead of us or whether we should try to backtrack and find some type of civilization.

We walked away from the accident as the sunlight began to fade, until we saw a nearby cluster of wood huts. As we approached the dwelling, we were feeling shook up and nervous. Sofia felt more so because she'd grown up in Africa and understood the dangers of the countryside.

I remember thinking, *I hope these people are friendly to outsiders.* I also hoped that any nearby predators, some of which prefer hunting for food at night, wouldn't consider us a nice change from their regular diets.

I was surprised. The people were warm and welcoming. They greeted us like something between long-lost relatives and gods visiting from the heavens. We explained what had happened and pointed to where we'd left the Jeep. They were very sympathetic and concerned.

"How do we get to the next big town?" I asked. "There is a coffee man," one of the men said. "He should be passing by at any time. He drives a big truck. He would probably be able to take you to Lobito."

Sure enough, in the distance, I spotted a pair of headlights. "Look!" I said to Sofia, pointing out the truck with much relief. But the lights abruptly disappeared! For a moment, I thought I must have just imagined it.

Shortly, the headlights reappeared. It was indeed the coffee truck. It had merely disappeared behind a hillside. As the vehicle bore down on the little cluster of huts, the residents gathered in the road near our Jeep and flagged the truck down.

The driver came to a stop and the locals explained the situation. "No problem," the driver said, using the traditional African response to almost every situation. "I can give you a ride." Eight of the villagers circled our Jeep and flipped it over, as I speechlessly looked on. They hoisted the Jeep onto the back of the truck, all before I could even offer to help.

We thanked our new friends, and headed off to Lobito on the coffee truck. We finally reached the city at about five o'clock in the morning. The driver let us off and we made arrangements for the wrecked Jeep.

My wife called her father, who said he would arrange for some of his friends to pick us up and bring us back to Luanda. I have to say that was a memorable honeymoon! I thought about how lucky I was to have met and married Sofia, as well as the amazing experiences in Africa. It was time to leave all the excitement behind and settle back into our new life in Bermuda.

This chapter of my life made me realize the importance of relationships, whether it was me with one of the chefs, the teamwork of the front and back of the house at the Princess, and especially with Sofia.

I had a newfound understanding about forming good, solid relationships with others. They were vital in both business and life. I had progressed so much in my career and personal life over the last couple of years. I was ready to see what was next.

My special recipe for you: The Original Caesar salad

This is the original Caesar salad recipe taught to my fellow staff member at the Princess hotel by Caesar Cardini himself. Our dining room captain, Antonio, met the famous chef at his restaurant in Mexico and asked him for the recipe.

When Antonio returned to Bermuda, he showed us how to prepare the famous salad. It was very popular at the Princess and at my restaurant.

There are many variations of this salad but this is the way Cardini prepared it.

Serving size: 4

Ingredients:

1 tablespoon chopped garlic

½ tablespoon Dijon mustard

3 anchovies

1 egg yolk

¼ cup vinegar

½ cup extra-virgin olive oil

Juice of 1 lemon

2 tablespoons Parmigiano Reggiano cheese

Romaine lettuce

Directions:

1. In a large bowl, use a fork to mash the garlic with the mustard, anchovies, and egg yolk until smooth.
2. Mix in the vinegar, then slowly add the olive oil while using a fork to blend the mixture until it is emulsified.
3. Add the lemon juice and cheese; toss the lettuce in the dressing.
4. Serve the salad on a cold plate.

Chapter 8: *Modifiche*

Changes

It was now 1971. I had been working at the Princess for about three years. Holiday Inn decide to compete in Bermuda's luxury accommodations market and opened a high-rise hotel at the other end of the island.

I applied there for a maître d' position, what I had been working for in the restaurant business for so many years. I had built my skills: learning different languages and cultures, studying various cuisines and cooking styles, and understanding how to provide refined service in an upscale restaurant.

Well, I finally achieved that goal: I was offered the position in the hotel's gourmet dining room. Several of us of us from the Princess ended up working there as maître d's or captains, and another of us was hired to be a manager.

My work in the gourmet room was very intense, involving preparing a number of tableside dishes—classics like steak Diane, pepper steak, Caesar and wilted spinach salads, and desserts such as zabaglione, crepes Suzette, and bananas flambé.

I immensely enjoyed preparing these dishes for the customers, as some involved a little showmanship like my friend's fruit salad creation. I also began teaching the tricks and techniques to less-experienced staff members. This teaching was just the start of something I would be doing for the rest of my restaurant career.

I was making fairly good money in Bermuda by then and had built up some cash reserves. Keeping it in the bank was okay, but the prospect of earning some money with my funds was a lure I couldn't pass up. I joined a number of others I knew who were investing in a mutual fund investment company, called Investors Overseas Service (IOS).

This company had been in business since 1955, employed over twenty-five thousand people, and had raised about $2.5 billion. IOS seemed stable and secure, and the opportunity didn't seem too risky to me. I was comfortable with the situation, so I invested about twenty thousand dollars.

The Swiss-based company, founded by international financier Bernard Cornfeld, began to experience financial difficulties due to stock market troubles; the share price of the publicly traded company continued to steadily drop.

An American backer, Robert Vesco, stepped in to help with the troubled company and took control. Vesco removed Cornfeld from management. He then siphoned off over two hundred million dollars in funds from IOS to cover his own investments, according to a public complaint issued against Vesco and some of his associates by the U.S. Securities and Exchange Commission (SEC).

Vesco fled the U.S. by company jet to Costa Rica. He proceeded to bounce around a number of countries, allegedly using bribery to keep the governments of those countries from extraditing him to the U.S. IOS collapsed and many investors, including myself, lost huge sums of money. Many banks in the U.S. and Europe were significantly impacted.

Cornfeld was arrested in Geneva and spent eleven months in jail before a judge acquitted him of fraud. I lost all but about fifteen hundred dollars due to the venture.

Once again, my hard-earned money was gone. Obviously, this was significantly more money than had been stolen from me in England and it deeply hurt my finances.

I was undeterred by my setback, though. I knew that investing was the way to build wealth, and I needed funds to continue the pursuit of my career. I decided to make an investment with more personal ties: I wanted to invest in real estate in southern Portugal. My wife's family had returned to Portugal after armed nationalist groups, seeking independence from the rule of Portugal, escalated their conflict with the Portuguese military forces stationed in Angola.

They had settled in the lovely city of Algarve, on the southern tip of the country's coast. Tourism was one of the booming industries in the area during the early seventies and many resort hotels were opening along the shoreline.

I saw this as a fantastic opportunity, so I contracted to buy three properties there with a new house to be built on each one. The deal was fifty percent down, another twenty-five percent halfway through construction, and the final twenty-five percent when the houses were completed.

One afternoon during late April 1974, I was helping set up for a big party in the hotel's main banquet room (built into what was left of the island's historic Fort St. George). The radio was on and the news announced a military coup d' état in Portugal.

The coup, centered in the country's capital of Lisbon, was a bloodless affair referred to as the Carnation Revolution. Leftist military forces toppled the country's authoritarian government of over forty years, Estado Novo, without firing a shot.

Otelo de Carvalho, considered the main architect of the revolution, was placed in command of a special military group and tasked with securing the country.

Portuguese citizens celebrated in the streets, with flowers being placed on soldiers' uniforms and in the barrels of rifles and cannons. While they celebrated, the revolution proved to be another financial disaster for me.

Turmoil began to brew in the country, as strikes broke out, media outlets were overtaken, the economy was disrupted, and land was seized. Some people began to panic, unsure of what would happen. Wealthy citizens fled the country, tourism dropped off, and corporations pulled their people and assets out of Portugal.

This impacted the company developing my properties and houses. With my investment at risk, I had to spend more money to hire an attorney. However, it was too late. The developer had already left Portugal. The attorney informed me there was nothing I could do and none of the investment could be recovered. I lost it all as the economic boom went bust.

Once again, forces conspired against me and I had lost money again. A common thief in England. A crooked investor from America. A political revolution in Portugal. The bottom line: my cash reserves were significantly diminished. Again. I wondered if I was not meant to have money. I wasn't poor anymore like in Italy, but something always seemed to happen when I had finally accumulated some funds.

It was a bitter pill for me to swallow. I had lost two large sums of money within a short period of time. Despite these financial setbacks, I knew I had to continue to make progress on my journey. This time, I decided to invest in myself. It was time to further improve my knowledge and gain official accreditation in the restaurant business.

I paid to enroll in a correspondence certificate program, sponsored by the Educational Institute of the American Hotel and Motel Association (now the American Hotel & Lodging Association). I selected four courses: Food and Beverage Management Service, Food and Beverage Controls, Introduction to Hotel-Motel Management, and Motel-Motor Hotel Management.

I took my studies seriously, completing all four courses between March 1974 and May 1975 and receiving my certifications. I was technically back in school, albeit correspondence classes. I made the most of my experience and was very focused on learning more about restaurant operations and management.

However, I was a little distracted; there was a big change happening in our lives. A new arrival was coming to the Molinaro family! Sofia found out she was pregnant in early 1974. We were ecstatic. Life was hectic though, between work and my studies, as we prepared for our little bundle of joy to arrive.

Along with the news of a new Molinaro joining the family, I heard that my father had passed away. He died on March 3, 1974— the same day my mama passed away in 1957. He lived seventeen years longer than my mama did. If only she could have lived that long.

The first week of September, Sofia went into labor. I took my wife to the hospital around midnight when the pains began. I spent the remainder of the night and all the next day with her. As sometimes happens with a first (and, in our case, only) child, delivery was difficult. The doctor finally said to me, "Listen, you might as well go home for a while. Nothing is happening." I was reluctant, but the doctor added, "We have given your wife something to induce labor, but it will take probably another seven or eight hours."

I didn't want to leave, despite the doctor's assurance. However, I went home and immediately fell into a deep asleep. Although I had just barely arrived back home and fallen sound asleep, I was shortly startled awake by the jangling of the telephone.

"Congratulations," the nurse on the phone said. "You have a beautiful baby girl." On September 6, 1974, after being in labor for two full days, Sofia gave birth to our daughter. We named our new daughter after her beautiful mother: Sofia Christina.

I jumped in my car and drove to the hospital as quickly as I could; it felt like a hundred miles an hour. I couldn't get there fast enough. When I arrived, I ran straight to the delivery room. My wife and baby were not there. They had already been moved.

I rushed excitedly to the nursery and identified myself, rushing over to the crib closest to me. I gazed down at the newborn, overwhelmed with emotion. "No, no," the nurse exclaimed, waving her hands. "It's the other one. Yours is in the next crib."

I laughed and looked down at the baby that really was mine. She was so beautiful, as beautiful to me as her mother always was. As fate would have it, I would not be the only one to mix up babies.

Two days later, a nurse entered my wife's room at feeding time with a baby in her arms. Sofia held her arms out for the baby and abruptly drew back. "This is not my baby!" The nurse looked startled but then apologized profusely. She hurried back to the nursery and this time returned with the real Sofia Christina.

Life on the island was good with our little family. It was a joyous time for us in those early months of Sofia Christina's life. I would put her in a stroller and take her down to the beach. As I ate ice cream, the tourists would gather around and fawn over her. "What a beautiful baby," they would say. She would look at all the people and contentedly coo.

It was also a crazy time. I was working, helping Sofia take care of our daughter, and taking courses to further my career. I had my head down and stayed busy. I was so absorbed in what my life had become, that I was insulated from what was happening around us on the island.

Our tiny island of Bermuda was not immune to the political discord of the turbulent seventies, as revolutions and unrest spread around the world. Just as Portugal and its former colonies and territories had erupted into conflict, so had our island paradise.

When I'd started working at Holiday Inn near the end of that season's summer tourism trade, Bermuda's police commissioner George Duckett was assassinated outside his home. Six months later, Governor Sir Richard Sharples and his aide were assassinated outside the Government House.

Riots broke out in the streets and violence escalated. A state of emergency was declared, with British military forces supplementing the police and civil authorities. Government officials tried to downplay all the violence and keep it out of the media, hoping to protect the crucial tourism trade. As with the upheaval in Portugal, residents began to leave the island.

The hotels, restaurants, and related businesses extensively relied on tourism, as did the government and the island's overall economy. Any drop-in tourism would have a ripple effect and significantly impact the island.

In the end, the government's attempts to suppress the news of the unrest proved impossible. Tourism was impacted and the number of visitors to the island dropped.

In the hotel business, we had tried not to pay much attention to the events swirling around us. Eventually, we couldn't ignore it any longer. We were worried about how the worsening situation would affect the hotel, and specifically our jobs.

There was a strict nighttime curfew in place. One night, I got caught on the beach after dark, which meant I couldn't risk being stopped on the road trying to get home. I was forced to spend the night on the beach, something that's truly not as much fun as it sounds to tourists.

Still, life on Bermuda was not all bleak. The hotel hosted a huge banquet for American Express, with about a thousand guests. It was a period-themed outdoor barbecue, on the nearby grounds of Fort St. George.

All the staff dressed up in ancient sea gear. I was dressed as a fifteenth-century ship's captain. A whole cow was roasted on a spit over an open fire pit. I was among those armed with knives to slice the roasted meat. It was a memorable occasion.

The political situation on Bermuda proceeded to deteriorate. The flow of people leaving the island continued. Business fell off at the hotel as tourism continued to take a hit. Our future on the island was uncertain with all the unrest. I began to think about moving my family, concerned about our welfare and safety. Paradise, I realized not for the first or last time, can indeed be lost.

The precarious situation, joined with other events in my life, made me seriously consider leaving. People I knew around the island in the hotel/restaurant industry began to leave for places like Canada, South Africa, Australia, and the United States.

A few of my friends at the hotel had returned home to Italy. I considered the option, as well. The more I thought about it, the idea started shaping up as my plan of escape. Finally returning to my homeland could be perfect for us.

However, fate was working overtime and had different plans for me, even if I didn't know it yet. We would be not heading east to my past, as I thought, but west to our future.

One of the Princess front desk managers, Eric H., had been hired by the Omni hotel chain to be their human resources manager. The hotel chain was scheduled to break ground on a hotel in Atlanta, Georgia, in fall 1975.

However, it proved difficult for him to find staff in Atlanta that was qualified to work in a five-star hotel. Humer asked his management if he could return to Bermuda and hire staff from there, since many of the hotel employees were leaving the island anyway. He got the green light and flew back to interview people.

He approached me and asked me to join him, but I said no. I was going back to Italy, I insisted to him; I had a plan. He pressed, saying he really wanted me to manage a restaurant at the hotel. The restaurant would be called Ristorante Bugatti. It was planned as a fine dining Italian restaurant, a then-unheard-of notion in the United

States. It would be branded around the Bugatti and decorated with photos of the exclusive Italian sports car.

Still I hesitated. "Look," he persisted, "we'll sign a contract for eighteen months, and then you can go back to Italy." I agreed to consider it. So, I went home and talked to Sofia.

After explaining the opportunity to her, she responded "Well, we have always wanted to visit the United States. And you would be managing a restaurant, not just going as a waiter. Let's go." With that, I put my plans for returning to Italy on hold and we started preparing our venture to the U.S.

This was my opportunity to significantly advance my career. I could put my management courses and certification to use. Also, it was imperative that I get my wife and daughter away from the tumultuous situation in Bermuda to safer living conditions.

I was conflicted in some ways. I really loved Bermuda and it would be hard to leave. However, the political and economic challenges were extremely concerning. I had a family now. I had to protect and provide for them.

I made the decision to leave. This would set me on a path to America, where my life would change in so many ways. Honestly, I would have stayed in Bermuda if the political and economic situation weren't in such an upheaval. I realize my life would have turned out very differently, though. I'm sure I would have never owned a restaurant and achieved the success I have.

With my mind made up, I headed to the American Consulate. I needed to find out what was required for us to pass through immigration. Much of the documentation was the same as required elsewhere: passport, birth certificate, health records, and criminal records for every country Sofia and I had lived in to date.

Certain forms had to be updated and all of them needed to be translated into English. Our daughter needed a passport, as well. Finally, I needed a written work offer from Omni. It took about a month to get all the documents in order, at which point I filed my visa application at the consulate.

It took five nerve-wracking months before I received notification that our visa application was approved. As a wonderful portent, the letter from the consulate arrived on Sofia Christina's first birthday. The necessary papers were waiting for us to pick them up.

I drove to the consulate to get the papers that would serve as my stepping stone off Bermuda and on to America. With the visa firmly in hand, I slid back behind the wheel of my car. I was so excited to get home and in such a rush, I took a corner too quickly. Well, you can guess what happened next: bang, crash, another accident.

I was okay, just mainly annoyed that the car crash delayed my return home. I finally arrived home and showed the letter to my wife. I picked up my daughter and spun her around. She giggled as I chanted, no doubt echoing many Italians before me, "We're going to America! We're going to America!" Sofia Christina looked at me, wide-eyed. Of course, she didn't understand why I was excited or what going to America even meant. It was a wonderful present for all of us that day, though.

"Let's go buy our airline tickets!" I told Sofia. America, the shining beacon to people all around the world, a symbol of hopes and dreams, would soon add three new immigrants: the Molinaro family. Our new destination would see the culmination of my career aspirations—my own restaurant. But I wasn't quite there yet.

My special recipe for you: Lobster fra Diavolo

I always think of the Aldo restaurant in Milan when I think of seafood. Bermuda always had a good variety of seafood. I enjoyed how fresh it was.

Serving size: 2

Ingredients:

1 2-lb. fresh whole lobster

2 oz. olive oil

Flour

1/2 cup of good-quality white wine

1 tablespoon garlic

Parsley

6 oz. can crushed tomatoes (pureed)

1 tablespoon of butter

Cayenne

Crushed red pepper

Salt and black pepper

Directions:

1. Finely chop the garlic and parsley.
2. Split the lobster in half starting at the head and working towards the tail.
3. In a large skillet, heat up the olive oil on medium heat.
4. Pass the lobster lightly through the flour.
5. Place the lobster in the skillet with the meat down and cook it for one minute.
6. Reduce heat to medium low.
7. Add the wine and cook for about 30 seconds.
8. Add the garlic and tomatoes then cook for 3 to 4 minutes on low heat.

9. Add the parsley and butter; then add salt and pepper, cayenne, and crushed red pepper to taste.

10. Cook for 5 minutes until the lobster shell turns red.

11. Serve the lobster with cappellini (thin spaghetti).

Chapter 9: *Arrivando in America*

Coming to America

Our upcoming move to the U.S. was becoming a reality. The land of opportunity beckoned. This was a dream come true for me. As a boy, I had wondered about what America was like as I watched the Westerns in our local Catholic church. Now, I would find out first-hand.

Eagerly, we packed up our home for the move, sorting through the many items we'd acquired or combined since becoming husband and wife on this beautiful yet troubled island. We sorted them into essential and non-essential piles. I'm sure the Italian explorers of old brought less with them that we were bringing.

A number of personal items, such as all the photos I had taken during all my travels, were in Europe. I had left them in Italy with my brother, who offered to keep two suitcases full of my stuff in his attic until we returned to collect them.

I packed up some boxes with our honeymoon keepsakes and other non-essential personal items, then shipped them to Atlanta. They were to arrive a few weeks before us in America. We packed everything we would need into our suitcases.

On October 15, 1975, Sofia and I caught a morning flight with our little Sofia Christina. She was about to take her first trip by airplane. We flew from Bermuda to JFK Airport in New York City. I watched the skyline as we made our approach for landing. This was it: we were landing in America, leaving the strife of Bermuda behind.

I would miss our paradise. Thinking back on what an amazing time we had on the island, I feel certain we would have stayed if the violence was not increasing. Of course, if I stayed I would never have had the opportunity to open my own restaurant. But America offered new challenges and new cuisine. I was ready.

We filed off the plane and were directed to immigration. An immigration officer waved us up and inspected our papers. He handed them back to me, along with a folder he presented that contained my green card. We now had lawful permanent residency. Unlike Bermuda, I wasn't required to purchase a return flight.

The officer shook my hand and said, "Welcome to America." I felt my breath catch in my throat. For a moment, I nearly burst into tears. I don't know if my sweet mama would have ever thought I would make it to America, about to embark on the next steps of my career. I was doing something none of my siblings had done, just as my mama had predicted.

This was such a dizzying moment. For every other country that I had entered, the immigration officers were very mechanical. They would scrutinize my papers to ensure everything was in order. Then, the officer would simply wave me on and turn his attention the next person before I was had turned away.

This felt like a sincere, warm welcome, like we mattered. It seemed like America was happy to open its shining gates to us. I found myself thinking *I want to be just like an American*. I was glad my English was fairly good, as was Sofia's. After all, it was our early discussions during English classes that led to our dating.

I threw my arms around Sofia, who was holding our daughter, and we hugged tightly. We turned and thanked the officer, who smiled and wished us good luck. We probably weren't the first, or the last, immigrants he had welcomed to the U.S., but we did feel special. It was a great start to our new life.

With this wondrous feeling, we went in search of our connecting flight to Atlanta. The airport was so big and buzzing with activity. In some ways the atmosphere felt familiar to the train station in Milan or other big cities in the early part of my travels. People bustled from one point to the next, conversing quietly or laughing at some amusing story.

But this was a new experience, America, and unlike Europe in so many ways. I soaked it all in, as did Sofia. Sofia Christina, only a toddler, was nonplussed about the whole experience. She didn't comprehend the magnitude of our journey and the new land we would call home.

We arrived in Atlanta, Georgia, and collected our bags. An Omni Hotel manager was waiting at the airport to greet us. He escorted us to our temporary lodgings at another hotel, which the Omni would provide for us until we found our own place.

Exhausted and a little overwhelmed, we settled into our new accommodations as best we could for the time being. The Omni was not yet open, so we had several free days to wander around and explore this city of the Old South that was now so passionate about leading the New South.

Like so many of the cities I'd been lucky enough to work in after leaving Italy, Atlanta was all about tomorrow: it was like the visions of the future presented by Disney. Sure, I'd heard a bit about the South, which glorified the old Atlanta in movies like *Gone with the Wind*.

But to Atlanta and its residents, that was then, this was now. The city, the capital of Georgia, was working overtime to outshine cities that clung to the past, places like

New Orleans, Mobile, or Savannah, to create a steel-and-glass leader of financial success.

Transportation, first the railroads and then the airport, fueled the growth of Atlanta. Its position in the Confederacy as a railroad hub led to its capture and many of its builds being burned by Union forces in 1864. The railroads, and the city, returned after the Civil War. Trade and commerce created prosperity and growth.

Following World War II, Atlanta began construction on new highways and freeways. The airport facilities were upgraded and it became one of the busiest hubs in the U.S. The city then turned its attention to tourism and convention business. A new entertainment and convention complex was constructed in the downtown area, including major sports facilities to go along with the hotels, restaurants, and businesses.

In this sprawling metropolis that was our new home, I realized we would need a vehicle to get around. So, one of the first things I did in America was buy a car. This was the American way, right?

As a restaurant manager-to-be, I expected to make a good salary. I decided to buy a new Mercury Monarch, a sedan that got good gas mileage. This was a new breed of "compact" luxury sedan that arose after the gas crisis of 1973. I hoped this car would treat me and my family better than other cars in my life had.

Next, it was time to find a place to live. We knew we didn't want to live in Atlanta. We wanted Sofia Christina to have some space to run around, as I did as a youth in Cerea. The hotel manager recommended we look in Norcross, a small town on the outskirts of Atlanta.

Norcross is located twenty miles northeast of Atlanta, with easy access to the city. It was a railroad town situated along the Eastern Continental Divide. The town was named for Jonathan Norcross, an early Atlanta mayor. Woods and streams nearby the town led to the area gaining a reputation as a resort community.

When we visited the town, the area reminded me of the classic American Westerns I had watched in movies while growing up. I was not the only Italian child enthralled by these films. In the 1960s, many Italian filmmakers paid homage to these types of movies and created a new, related genre: "Spaghetti Westerns." These movies (many of them filmed in Spain) became popular around the world. Hollywood actors such as Clint Eastwood and Charles Bronson starred in such films.

So, those movies played through my mind when I saw Norcross for the first time. There was a railway station, a scattering of homes, and vast empty fields. The sight of the railway station took me back to the one in Sanguinetto, naturally.

Also, I was astonished to even see cowboys on horseback, or at least people wearing cowboy hats as they rode. It was like they had ridden off the silver screen into real life. I was glad no one had any six shooters on them!

We fell in love with the town immediately. There were several newly built apartment complexes, the hotel manager told us. Many of the apartments were still under construction, but a few were available for rent. We looked around and found a nice one we liked. We signed the papers and were told we could move in a few days later.

I went to the freight office to pick up our boxes from Bermuda. As we were unpacking, I realized one box was missing. I rushed back to the freight office, but they could not locate it. I was devastated. The lost box contained all of our photos from our wedding and the honeymoon trip, including the animals we had seen in Africa. Other missing photos were ones I had taken in Portugal and Bermuda. The worst was that we'd lost all of Sofia Christina's baby pictures.

We were really sad about losing these treasured photographs. They were irreplaceable. And, to my undying sadness, I got more bad news some years later about all the photos my brother was keeping for me in Italy; when I returned for a visit, my brother told me that all the collected photos I had left with him in two suitcases were ruined by the humidity in his attic.

"They were up there a very long time," he shrugged, by way of apology. All I had left of all those countries I had visited, all the travel, were only memories in my mind and, ultimately, in my heart. I'm still heart-broken over the lost memories.

As the date of the Omni Hotel's grand opening approached, the management organized a staff meeting for all the new hires. The meeting began with a tour of the hotel. I had already familiarized myself with the other downtown hotels, and this was built in a similar style to the city's Hyatt Regency, featuring an atrium in the style that Hyatt had made its signature look.

The Omni had interior balconies, flowers everywhere, and a spacious elevator in the lobby. In the center of the ground floor, there was an intimate French restaurant. Its chef had previously worked on the luxurious French Line ship *Normandy*, one of the most famous liners to ever ply the Atlantic.

When the comprehensive tour concluded, we ate lunch with the hotel's management team. Following lunch, we were escorted to a banquet room for the meeting describing all the rules, duties, regulations, and shift information.

Then, each new employee's job assignment was announced. I proudly waited for my name to be called as the manager of the Ristorante Bugatti. The position was an important one, as it would offer a fine Italian dining experience in the hotel.

When they called my name, I sat there, stunned. I didn't get the manager position. I was told I was a maître d'. What had happened? I came to America because of the opportunity to manage a restaurant. After the initial shock wore off, I wanted to jump up and protest. It took discipline not to, though. My mama's advice, given all those years ago, won out.

Good thing, too. I was scared that if I refused the maître d' position, I would be out of a job in a very large country where I hardly knew anyone. I was planning my return to Italy before Omni and my HR contact had detoured me. It was the opportunity to take the manager's position that made me travel all this way.

So what could I do for now? Nothing but hold my tongue and bite my lip. I sat in silence and watched as they called out the name Sergio as the Ristorante Bugatti manager. I knew Sergio. We had worked together at the Princess, along with Andrea who had been a cook.

Sergio was a nice enough guy but he had never managed a restaurant to my knowledge; also, he hadn't taken any courses in hotel restaurant management, like I had. I was confident that I was far more qualified. So what got him the job over me?

Andrea, sitting next to me, saw my disappointment and tried his best to cheer me up. "I don't understand it," I kept saying. "That job was supposed to be mine. What did I do that they demoted me? They promised me I would be the manager. It's in the letter they sent me."

Andrea looked at me sympathetically. "You did nothing wrong," he said. "I happen to know the reason. They chose Sergio simply because he is much taller than you are. He's a tall, very handsome man, and they thought he would make a good impression standing at the door of their restaurant."

I thought back to the Biffi in Milan, where I was told I could never be a waiter there. The reason? Because I didn't meet the minimum height requirement. I was six inches too short. Once again, my ability to do a job I really wanted had come down to my height. On this point, America was proving to be no better than Italy.

Well, time to do what I had done every time I faced a setback in my life. I have had so many, that it toughened me up. I just faced the situation and decided to make the best of it. I told myself since I cannot do anything about not being offered the manager's position, I would accept the maître d' job and move on.

I knew that there would be other opportunities at hotels or restaurants, especially here in America. For now, I reminded myself to learn everything I can about the business and America, this terra incognita as the Romans would say.

One of my favorite movies, released in 1974, is *Pane e cioccolata*, or *Bread and Chocolate*. It is an award-winning Italian comedy/drama that follows an Italian immigrant to Switzerland. The protagonist, Nino, becomes a "guest worker" as a waiter in Switzerland. He loses his work permit after a minor infraction of the law. He goes into hiding so he isn't forced to leave the country. He dyes his hair blond and attempts to fit in with the locals. He is discovered and sent back to Italy.

That's how I felt in many ways. My mama told me that respect and discipline were two traits that would serve me well. Like Nino, I wanted to fit in like a local. The best way to do that was to discover the culture and immerse myself in it. I wasn't going to dye my hair blond, though.

I began to explore the strange new world around me, as I previously had ventured through streets of Milan, Frankfurt, London, and Hamilton, Bermuda. I would learn the culture and find out how the English I had learned differed in America.

For all the happiness I felt with my family, American was proving to be so different to me. Atlanta and our new home in Norcross took some getting used to. The weather was different, with lots of heat and humidity. I had to learn the many idioms and expressions unique to America (so very different than the English I learned and spoke in Britain and Bermuda). Also, the food was different (especially Southern food). Lots of foods were deep fried and covered in gravy.

One aspect of Atlanta that I really liked was the business environment. The city of Atlanta I experienced (in terms of the clientele I met at the new Omni) was the most forward-thinking city I'd lived and worked in so far. It would prove, I realized later, to be the perfect introduction to Houston, Texas. Both cities were similar in terms of economy and growth.

The grand opening of the hotel took place on November 7, 1975. The mayor of Atlanta attended, since the Omni represented the city's attitude and spirit as it grew and changed. The hotel also represented the investment of millions of dollars, something that mayors always like.

The Ristorante Bugatti's grand opening would take place the following day. There were several dishes on the menu that required the classic tableside preparation. I was very comfortable, having done this for many years. But I found out that most of the waiters on staff had never been trained to do this. It was up to me to teach them.

Starting a few days before the opening, Chef Andrea and I began training the waiters. We had them come in early every day, an hour before their shift started, to practice. Despite our best efforts—all the time, patience, and training—we had to limit the tableside preparation. The waiters were not interested in food preparation. They simply wanted to carry completed dishes to tables.

We decided to offer just two savory dishes (brandy pepper steak and steak Diane) and one dessert (zabaglione). Now, making zabaglione isn't rocket science, but it is challenging. It requires only two to three minutes of intense whipping over a moderate heat source to blend the sugar, egg yolks, and a splash of marsala wine from Sicily.

It is a delicate dance between creating the ideal thick, foamy, warm consistency and overcooking the eggs. If you're not careful, you can create a curdled mess you cannot serve to anyone. Many of the waiters, however, could never master this dish. After a while, we had to stop offering zabaglione.

At the Omni, business was not meeting the projections for the first few months. Management, eager to do something to boost the numbers, hired a group of musicians to perform most nights at the hotel's supper club. The group called themselves The Gypsies. They came all the way to Atlanta from Houston, eight hundred miles away, to play.

One day I was eating lunch with the band's leader, Greg Harbar, whom I had befriended. During our meal, I mentioned to him how bad business was. He simply chuckled and said, "If it's gold you want, you should move to Houston." I smiled, assuming he was joking.

If it was so good in Houston, I countered, what was he doing here, in Atlanta? "Seriously," he explained, "Houston is the oil capital, the country's energy capital. Surely you've heard of Texas oil?"

I shrugged. I had no plans to leave Atlanta. But I would soon leave the Omni. After nearly eight months, I was ready to leave so I accepted a position at one of the Omni's competing hotels in Atlanta, the Hilton.

I finally had an offer, a solid offer, to manage a restaurant. The Hilton offered me the job of managing the Café de la Paix. The pay wasn't great, but I was eager for a change. And this was the chance to oversee the restaurant's operation and put my training and skills to work.

After starting at the Hilton, I suggested to Sofia one day that she and our daughter, who was nearly two by then, come by to see the Café. I was proud and wanted to show them where I worked. We piled into the car and headed out.

We exited the freeway and headed downtown. At the intersection ahead, the light had just turned green. There were no cars in front of me, so I cruised on. Midway through the intersection, a Postal Service truck ran the red light to our left and smashed into us. Another accident, and this time with my family in the car!

My wife, who was sitting with Sofia Christina on her lap (this was prior to the requirement of car seats for small children), assured me they were all right. Thank God. I turned to see the other vehicle speeding away.

Leaping out of the car, I started to chase him down the street. He had no intention of stopping and I quickly lost him. The police arrived and took a report. Because the other driver did not stop, that meant I was responsible for paying for all the damages to my car.

I could not escape the bad luck with accidents; it was still following me. At least my precious cargo was not injured, nor was I. Fortunately, the car was still drivable, so I climbed back behind the wheel and we continued on to the café.

My wife loved the place. The restaurant, as its name reflected, was French. Pictures of Paris hung on the walls, depicting familiar scenes such as the Eiffel Tower, the Arc de Triomphe, and its most famous avenue, the Champs-Élysées.

I was comfortable with the cuisine and the style of service the restaurant should provide, but from the first day I had problems with the staff. They were not trained well at all. I met with hotel management to discuss ways to tackle this problem. The recommendation was that the staff and I come in an hour early every other day, so I could train them.

I was happy to do so, figuring a role of teacher was now part of my job description. I was excited and ready to help the staff learn new things, as I had been so eager to do in my career. I also reflected about the many people who had taught me so much over the years. Some were formal teachers, but most gave me real-world, on-the-job learning experiences. I was grateful for them and ready to help my staff as they learned.

However, this proved to be most challenging and very vexing to me. The staff was uncooperative and we made little progress. I became unhappy and frustrated. I could not fathom why anybody would not want to learn, given the opportunity. Honestly, I could never understand this. It would cost me a lot of peace and happiness now, as well as in the later years of my career.

Still, I carried on and always did my very best. I trained them on a variety of tasks and skill they needed; it was to no avail. I encouraged them, I cajoled them, I implored them. Nothing worked. They did not cooperate or see the value in what I was teaching them. I could not force or coerce my employees to understand that the knowledge and skills would benefit their future and their earning potential.

I wanted to show them some simple ideas, based on my own experience, career, and life. But my effort was a waste of time. They were simply not interested in learning. This was not how I saw my career. I decided that even though I was now a manager, this was not the situation I wanted or needed at this point in my life. Once again, I began to look around for new opportunities.

My special recipe for you: Zabaglione

I would make this dessert tableside at the Ristorante Bugatti. It's a very simple, yet rich, dish. I haven't seen any restaurants offering this dish in a long time.

It's great to make as the culmination of an intimate dining experience at home. This dish is versatile; it can also be used as a sweet sauce with another dessert or even frozen.

You might want to practice some before you try it for your guests, though, to make sure you can get the consistency right.

Serving size: 2

Ingredients:

2 egg yolks

2-1/2 tablespoons white sugar

3 oz. sweet marsala wine (not dry)

Chocolate powder or pieces of fresh fruit

Directions:

1. Place all the ingredients in a stainless-steel bowl. Firmly grip the bowl with one hand and hold the bowl over an open flame.

2. After about 45 seconds, whisk the ingredients in a clockwise motion as quickly as you can until they are thick and foamy; the consistency should be pudding-like.

3. Remove the bowl from the flame and dish several ounces or more into a cup. Sprinkle a little chocolate powder on top or add fresh fruit pieces.

4. You can serve this dish warm right away or chill it first.

Chapter 10: *Citta di Asta*

Boomtown

I continued my fruitless effort to train the staff for several months. I was beyond the point of frustration when I got a fateful phone call. Eric H., the HR representative that had convinced me to come to America to work for the Omni, had moved on to a hotel in Houston.

He was working at the Warwick, a very famous and storied hotel built in 1926. He wanted me to join him there, asking me to become the food and beverage manager. I turned him down, saying I should stay in Atlanta. He persisted, calling several more times. Each time would listen to his pitch then politely refused.

Eric was not dissuaded though. The next time I heard from him, he sent a letter including an airplane ticket to Houston. He really wanted me to visit, to see the hotel and Houston for myself, before I made up my mind about the position for good.

Well, it wouldn't hurt to just take a look, I decided, since Eric went to all the trouble and expense to buy me a ticket. I also thought back to what Greg Harbar, my friend and the leader of The Gypsies, had told me about Houston: it was an energy boomtown.

So I reached out to Greg and asked for more information on Houston, to see what he and his bandmates knew about the Warwick. What I heard from them intrigued me, so I decided to take Eric up on the trip offer.

Dressed in one of my best suits, I flew to Houston and met with Eric at the hotel. He described the responsibilities of the food and beverage manager, which interested me. However, the salary he offered was not attractive to me. It was around twelve hundred dollars a month.

We spent considerable time talking about what possibilities existed to move up the ladder at the Warwick. I thanked him for the ticket and we concluded the meeting. I told him I would like a few days to decide.

I couldn't get over the salary I was offered. It was not what I was expecting, especially to uproot my family and move from Atlanta to Houston. Although the position was a step up, the pay was not. When I stepped outside the hotel that late morning, Greg was standing there, expectantly waiting for me.

We went to lunch and I told Greg that although I liked what I had seen of Houston, the salary wasn't enough to make it worth relocating there. He had some ideas. Since I was already in Houston, he suggested, "Let's check out a few places I know and get a sense of what else is out there."

I agreed, so we started to drive around some other parts of Houston. He took me to a place on Post Oak Boulevard near The Galleria, called Tony's. The restaurant was considered the best in all of Houston. I asked to speak to the manager and was told there were no openings.

So off we went to the next restaurant, called Le Pavilion, not too far from Tony's. I remembered reading a review for this place while I was still in Bermuda. The manager there, another Carlo (Morelli), told me that if I was a really good waiter and could sell the daily special, I could make six or seven hundred dollars a week. *That much? Per week?* The Warwick had just offered me twelve hundred dollars a month, less than half that.

In total disbelief, all I could stutter was, "When can I start?" Carlo replied "You can start Monday, if you like." I promised him I'd be back as soon as I could and jumped on the next flight to Atlanta. Greg was right, and I was thankful he had wanted to take me around, prospecting for another opportunity.

When I arrived home, I told Sofia excitedly that I had, indeed, found gold in Houston. Although I would be back to waiting on tables, I could make a lot of money doing so. She agreed with me about accepting the offer and we starting preparing to make the move from Atlanta to Houston. Sofia Christina was not in school yet, and we had no real ties to Atlanta. We hurriedly packed our essentials and arranged to ship our remaining belongings.

I let Eric know that I appreciated his offer, but I politely declined. Unfortunately, his plan had backfired. I came to Houston to listen to his pitch yet accepted a different job. I would have loved to work at the Warwick if the salary was better.

Driving the eight hundred miles west to Houston would give us a chance to see some of the countryside. We piled into the car and set off for the Texas boomtown. A song came on the radio and we began to laugh and sing along. The song? It has become one of my favorites, and almost a theme song for my life to that point: Willie Nelson's

"On the Road Again." It struck me on such a personal note. Did he know my story? That was a great introduction to country music for me.

We arrived in Houston and found a place to stay. I started work at Le Pavilion on Monday, just as Carlo had offered. In 1974, Carlo had purchased the restaurant, modeled after New York's acclaimed restaurant of the same name; it was the area's first four-star French restaurant.

The menu primarily featured French cuisine, but dishes changed substantially every day. Carlo had said during our first discussion that selling the daily special was vital to the job. It was true. If we wanted to keep our jobs, we were told, we had to push the daily specials.

These specials were very expensive. Since they were not listed on the menu, customers never knew how expensive until they got the bill. There was a method to Morelli's tactic. The diners paid their bills without blinking. It was, after all, Boomtown Houston.

I worked hard and did well. But three months into the job, the manager informed us that the restaurant was closing. There was talk that the landlord had received a lucrative offer for the real estate. He had, no doubt, offered to buy out the remainder of the restaurant's lease. This was common in Houston at that time, since the economy was surging and prime real estate was pure gold.

In January 1978, Le Pavilion hosted its last party. The celebration honored of the inauguration of Bill Clements as governor of Texas. The restaurant went out with a bang, then closed its doors for the final time. I was out of a job. Houston's real estate market made millionaires, but left me on the street.

Immediately I went out looking for work along with Daniel, a friend I'd made at the restaurant. We applied at an Italian-American place, Rudy's Restaurant, and to our surprise they hired both of us. "Finally, I'm getting some professional waiters!" manager John Puglia told us. My unemployment was over as quickly as it began.

A few weeks later, Daniel approached me during our shift. "See those two men at my table over there?" he said, nodding to direct my gaze. "They run a top steakhouse in New York City and they're planning to open another one here, over on Westheimer."

The restaurant was to be The Palm, whose sister restaurant is an iconic, high-end steakhouse that first opened in New York City in 1926. The original restaurant is known not only for its food, but also its caricatures and cartoons of celebrities, city scenes, and local happenings.

I listened, curious about what had attracted his interest. I soon found out. "A waiter there can easily make fifty to sixty thousand a year!" he gushed. I laughed. No waiter made that much money. But he was insistent. "Let's go, Carlo," he urged. "Let's apply!"

His enthusiasm, and mine, was tempered some when he admitted the likelihood of landing a job was slim. He said, "They typically bring staff from their other restaurants in New York and elsewhere to fill the best positions. "He related a story about a friend who once offered fifteen thousand dollars to one of the restaurant's waiters, who was leaving, if he could replace him. The restaurant brought in someone from within to take the place of the departing waiter.

That stunned me. "Still, it's worth a shot," Daniel said. Finally I agreed. Of course, we didn't get an offer. I wasn't surprised, though, but being turned down was still a real letdown. However, I started pondering what it would be like to make that kind of money. Unable to get the idea out of my head, I returned two weeks later and applied again. And again, I was turned down.

Over the following weeks, the idea of all that money occupied my thoughts. It would not leave my head. Almost every waking minute, my brain would return to consider the seemingly inconceivable possibility of earning that much money.

I thought about how that money could help create a financial stability for my family we had not previously experienced. I could also make sure that Sofia Christina would be better off than I ever dreamed to be as a child. The prospect of earning that kind of money was what had drawn me to America.

I was going to make this happen. Persistence had always been one of my strong points, so I decided to try again. I gathered all my work references together, dressed sharply, and headed back to The Palm. Timing my arrival to coincide with the end of the lunch rush, I asked to speak to the assistant manager, John B.

I greeted John with a big smile, handing him my folder of reference letters. He glanced through the folder and looked at me with regret. He took in all my experience and said, "I'm afraid we're not looking for a restaurant manager." "Oh, no," I quickly responded, "I was hoping for a job as a waiter." He looked at me, glancing through the folder's contents again.

"Wait here. Let me go speak to the manager and see if there is anything available," John said. He crossed the room and quietly spoke to the manager, who had his back to me. I stood and waited, trying to look cool and professional, not like the chained elephant I felt like. I did not want to look too excited or appear too eager.

I saw the manager turn, look at me, and say something. At this point, the assistant manager walked back in my direction. I held my breath. "Can you start right away?" I didn't hesitate. I was beside myself—I got the job! Visions of dollar signs danced in my head.

"Let's get you a uniform," John said. He led the way to a back room, sifting through a collection of beige jackets until he found one that would fit me. "We'll talk more tomorrow about the details the job," he explained. "Just dress casually, since the restaurant doesn't open for a few more days."

The grand opening of The Palm in Houston was set for August 5, 1978. I couldn't wait to get home and share the good news with Sofia. Our fortunes in Houston were about to greatly improve. I was about to earn my share of the money flowing through Houston.

The following day, I wanted to make a good impression so I arrived early. The assistant manager, at this point my hero, led me into the dining room. Several young men were busy organizing the place. He pointed toward a bucket and a sponge. "Start by cleaning all the dust from the booths and benches," he told me.

I was surprised and more than a little disappointed to arrive as a waiter and instead be handed cleaning supplies. I wasn't immune to hard work though, and the others were diligently taking care of their organization and cleaning chores. I wanted to prove I could be a good team player, so I got to work on the booths and benches.

Three days later, The Palm opened. The service wasn't as fancy as I had anticipated. There was no tableside preparation, since all the food came out of the kitchen already plated up. The food, in fact, was to me surprisingly simple: Italian-American fare alongside the steaks for which the restaurant was famous.

The food was straightforward and well prepared. Coupled with the excellent reputation of its New York City sibling, the place quickly became quite popular. It was especially popular with certain well-to-do, high-living patrons who were gravitating to the nearby, exclusive Tanglewood neighborhood.

Daniel had been right. I was making great money. Also, I met some very important people, like Mark White. He was a prominent Texas lawyer who would become Governor of Texas in five years. I became his favorite waiter at The Palm.

I would sometimes offer my customers items that were not on the menu, dishes I could easily prepare. I promised the chef a portion of my tips if he let me do some cooking when I had a special customer in my section.

This approach worked well with the chefs on staff. It was costing me more than the bottles of wine I used to provide to the chefs for letting me watch them in action. But it was totally worth it. However, one chef, Carlo Bruno, resisted and resented me at the start. I poured on the big smile and charm, not to mention some money from my tips for him. I also offered him something else: knowledge.

Chef Bruno finally relented after hearing about what I had in mind—my proposed exchange of knowledge. I would teach him some traditional Italian dishes and he would let me cook and give me pointers. In the process, I could make my customers very happy. Which meant bigger tips for me. Which meant a bigger payoff to him. We both won by him letting me come into the kitchen and cook.

One of my regular customers was a gentleman from Hawaii who always came in by himself. He would typically ask to start with my Caesar salad, which I'd learned to prepare in Bermuda. The iconic salad became so popular with our clientele that the assistant manager asked if I would show the pantry cook how to make the dressing. I felt very proud when Caesar salad was later added to The Palm's a la carte menu.

At The Palm, I noticed some waiters were unhappy when a customer sat alone in their station. It was more work for less money they complained, because it is as easy to cover a table of two as it is for one. But I felt more responsibility with a lone customer.

When you sit down to eat with a group of other people, they entertain you. A single diner might welcome a little conversation, beyond asking them what they would like to eat and drink. I made an extra effort for these customers.

I would ask such customers if they'd like me to make something off the menu for them, for instance a simple dish like risotto. Often enough, they were intrigued by the special dish and very appreciative. In the end, they turned out to be some of the best-tipping customers I, or any other waiter, could hope to have.

Soon, a number of these solo customers began to request me. Some would say, "Carlo, make for me whatever you think is best." And I would. The Hawaiian gentleman was one of these. He was a generous tipper, always giving me fifty dollars no matter what the bill amount was.

He told me he made his money selling a piece of family land in Hawaii to the Hilton Hotels for several million dollars. Now, he sold lithographs. The man finished every meal with a glass of Louis XIII Cognac, perhaps the best cognac in the world and arguably the most expensive.

Even in those days, Louis XIII could cost around seventy-five dollars a snifter. Today, it would probably run you closer to three hundred dollars. He always paid cash, which he always carried a lot of. When he opened his wallet, all the hundred-dollar bills would fan out like an accordion. While he wasn't ostentatious about it, he didn't try to hide it either.

One evening he came into The Palm and had a drink at the bar, joining many well-dressed patrons who treated this as their nightly home away from home. After he paid for his drink, he headed into the men's room.

Moments later, he burst out of the bathroom in a panic, shouting that he'd just been robbed. Someone had held a gun to his head and demanded his wallet.

He ran out of the restaurant before anyone could investigate or call the police. To my disappointment, I never saw him again.

Still, if word of the bathroom robbery got around, it certainly didn't affect the restaurant's popularity. The place was always packed with business people, especially those in the oil business. This was a familiar character type around Houston. While many customers in the oil business were not loud, pushy, and boastful with money, many of them fit the cliché perfectly.

Some nights, I felt like I was taking care of people not in Houston but in a *movie about Houston*. Here I was, back to thinking of my life as a movie. This role was not one I enjoyed playing, though.

The stereotypical oilmen who came in would offer me extra money to hook them up with single ladies at the bar. This sort of thing fit right in at The Palm, which became known as something of a pickup place for single and married alike. It was not really my job, but there was an unspoken expectation. The men would slip me fifty or a hundred dollars to arrange an introduction to one of the ladies. I wasn't proud of this.

Over the next several years of working at The Palm, I continued to do well. However, I couldn't understand the restaurant's overwhelming popularity with its casual service and simple food. It was difficult for me to reconcile this, after working in so many fine dining establishments.

I wondered how and why it was this way, but soon I came to understand this was the way of America and especially Houston.

In response to seeing so much success for so little actual achievement, I began to envision opening a restaurant of my own. There were a number of restaurants in Houston serving Italian fare, but they actually were all were Italian-American.

The dishes they served were the American take on Italian food, just like Mexican and Chinese food in America looks and tastes nothing like cooking in their countries of origin. Almost no restaurants did tableside preparation either, beyond the occasional flambé like bananas foster or crêpe Suzette at dessert time.

I was from Italy. I had first learned to cook in Italy, from the chef in a premier restaurant. And I had been introducing certain authentic Italian dishes at The Palm, like zabaglione, risotto, and osso buco. They were wildly popular with the diners.

I started thinking about this night and day, turning it over in my mind. *Shouldn't I do this at my own place, instead of someone else's?* I had been in the restaurant business for over two decades. I had learned so much but was ready for a new challenge.

I thought of the advice my mama had given me: "Do your best all the time and you will go far in life." I decided to add to her wisdom. "Do your best all the time and money will follow." I was doing my best and making good money. But with my own restaurant, I could do better. And make more money.

I made the decision; it was time for me to own a restaurant. Sofia encouraged me to take the big risk if it felt right to me. So, with every waking moment I was not busy at The Palm, I started looking around. In 1983, I found a restaurant, suggestively called *Gigolo*, not too far from The Palm.

The owner wanted to move to Austin to be near her daughter. She was ready to move on and we negotiated a price of around twenty thousand dollars. Only one hurdle remained. I would need approval from the owner of the shopping center, Weingarten Realty.

Weingarten is a Houston-based company that owns and manages a large number of shopping centers around the country. I wanted to take over the existing lease for the restaurant, so I wasted no time. I eagerly contacted a representative with the office to make an appointment.

With a meeting arranged, I brought copies of my financial records and professional history, as requested. I was told I would be contacted shortly. I left, unsure of what to expect. A week later, I was notified I had been turned down because I lacked any experience owning and running my own restaurant.

Disappointed, I went back to Gigolo and told the owner that our deal was off. She thought for a moment then explained, "There might be another way." I was intrigued and asked her to continue. She said my old friend Daniel, who had originally steered me to the Palm Restaurant, had opened his own restaurant a couple of years before. What a crazy, small world. Here Daniel was coming back into my life.

Daniel was struggling financially, the owner confided. The root of his troubles lay with his young son's medical condition. His son had stopped breathing shortly after birth but the doctors had managed to resuscitate him. Ever since then, the infant had been suffering health problems.

As it turned out, Daniel had borrowed money from her. Now, he wanted to take his family to Canada because a doctor there specialized in treating conditions like his son's. He might be willing to sell his restaurant to me if I paid off his debt, the woman said.

By looking out for Daniel's family, and herself, she was in essence looking out for me. I went to see the place and spoke to Daniel. The restaurant was badly rundown by this point. Seeing the kitchen, I knew right away that it was simply too small for anything I had in mind. It would require a lot of remodeling. But I could see the potential in it, given some care and attention. And money.

Daniel's lease had four years left on it, at a cost of twenty-two hundred dollars a month. That seemed reasonable to me, given the time and place in Houston. We came to an agreement that I would pay off his debt to the owner of Gigolo and he would sign the lease over to me.

This was what we would say in Italian: "*Capita a fagiolo*." Translated into English, it literally means "occurs (or happens) at the bean." It figuratively means something took place at exactly the right moment. I suppose the phrase refers to hard times when food (beans) were available to keep a person from starving.

It had finally happened. Exactly when it needed to happen. The moment I had worked for my entire life was upon me. The only thing was, I wished my mama was there to see what I had accomplished on my long journey. Here in America, I had become a restaurant owner.

My special recipe for you: Steak Medallions with Balsamic

The Palm is known for its steaks. My steak medallions recipe is a tribute to the restaurant and the wonderful time I spent there.

Start with a high-quality cut of beef tenderloin, then slice two-inch steaks (about 8 oz.) across the meat's grain; this steak is referred to as filet mignon.

Serves: 2

Ingredients:

2 8-oz. filet mignon

1 cup high-quality red wine

½ cup balsamic vinegar

Fresh garlic gloves

1½ teaspoon Dijon mustard

Butter

½ tablespoon Italian parsley

2 tablespoons olive oil

Flour

Salt and pepper to taste

Directions:

1. Finely chop the Italian parsley and slice garlic cloves thinly into 8 pieces.
2. Drizzle the olive oil into a stainless-steel pan and heat over medium-high heat.
3. When the oil is hot, sear each filet mignon on both sides
4. Remove the filets from the pan and drain off some of the oil.
5. Add the garlic to the pan; when it begins to turn brown, add the mustard, red wine, and balsamic. Stir while cooking for 1 minute.
6. Add the butter and parsley, and salt and pepper to taste. Continue stirring while cooking the sauce for around one to two more minutes.
7. Return the filets to the pan and cook to the desired doneness.
8. Add the flour to the sauce and stir until thick.
9. Plate the filet mignon and pour the sauce over the top.

Chapter 11: *Il Sogno Realizzato*

The Dream Realized

Well, I now owned a restaurant. I had been preparing and working towards this all my life. I couldn't believe it was finally happening. I was so thrilled and ready to get the restaurant up and running, to welcome those first customers through the door.

That wouldn't happen right away, though. The reality was there was a lot to do before I could even think of opening. It was time to roll up my sleeves and get to work. I applied for all the necessary permits, figuring that with my background in furniture I could do most of the dining room remodeling myself.

I wanted to expand the kitchen workspace by moving its wall out four feet. I didn't have those types of skills, so I hired a construction company to perform the work. Deals in Texas those days were often done on nothing more than a verbal agreement and a handshake. The builder and I settled on five thousand dollars up front to complete the job; he agreed to finish the job in ten days.

Those ten days came and went and the work was not completed. Instead, the builder demanded an additional two thousand dollars. When I refused and reminded him of our agreement, he packed his tools and left. I would have to find someone else to move the wall.

Five years later, I ended up in court with the original builder. By that time, the once booming Houston economy was now in bad shape. The construction company had gone out of business and the judge ruled against my claim. I learned my lesson and have never relied upon a verbal agreement since. Another expensive lesson for me.

I finally hired a new company to complete the kitchen job, this time with a written agreement in place. When the work was done, I set out to design the dining room walls with panels depicting various scenes from Italy: Milan's Galleria, the canals of Venice, my Verona, and the scenic coastal town of Portofino.

The scene from Verona portrayed the fabled house of the Capulets from Shakespeare's *Romeo and Juliet*. For Portofino, the scene illustrated the colorful buildings that line the shore, as depicted on thousands of postcards. The restaurant entrance featured a beautiful map of seventeenth-century Italy.

I installed a rich, deep red carpet that matched the upholstery on the bistro chairs that surrounded tables draped in white linens. I wanted to keep my restaurant simple and focused on the customer, thus I kept the dining area modest with only twelve tables (four tops, so I could seat forty-eight guests).

The restaurant was shaping up, but it still wasn't ready. It was almost there. However, I ran out of money before my planned transformation was completed. I went to see my banker for a loan. When I'd first arrived in Houston, I visited several banks to try to open an account.

This was in the 1970s and there was no such thing as online banking or the kinds of banking conveniences we enjoy today. All of the banks had turned me away because I didn't have a permanent address yet. The Catch-22 was I needed a local bank account to get a place to live.

But when I went to one banker, Gary Karter, he saw no such obstacles with me being new to the city. We developed such a good relationship over the years that when he moved to a new bank, I moved my account so I could continue do business with him. He knew me, I knew him, and business runs on these types of relationships.

"I know this is my first restaurant," I told Gary, "but I will work hard and pay the money back, I promise." Gary smiled, looking confident. "I know you're good for it, Carlo. And I know that if the restaurant doesn't succeed, you'll find a way to pay me back, even if it means going back to The Palm as a waiter."

Like I said, he knew me pretty well. I would not rest until I paid every dime back, no matter what it took. We shook hands. Later, he provided me with paperwork to sign and I got the loan I needed. I could complete the renovations and prepare for the opening.

Now, I had to create the menu. I wanted the menu to be traditional, to represent the very best that Italy has to offer, especially since the other restaurants I had checked out in Houston served Italian-American dishes. This was the kind of food most Americans associated with Italian, lots of pastas with heavy cream sauces or thick red sauces.

Not in my restaurant, I vowed. I set out to create and reflect what I knew as real Italian food from my region back home. Dishes I had watched my mother prepare, from fresh ingredients. Elegant, yet unpretentious meals I had learned from chefs in Europe. Ideas I had gathered during my twenty-plus years in the restaurant business. Delicious, simple fare that celebrated my homeland, heritage, and most importantly, my family.

I chose my items for the menu carefully, serving dishes such as *penne ai tre pepperoni* (penne pasta with three pepper sauce, which happens to be my daughter's favorite), *veal scaloppini al limone* (thin veal slices with lemon), seafood salad (inspired by the Aldo restaurant), *fettucine alla Bolognese* (fettucine pasta with a light tomato and meat sauce), tiramisu (a coffee-flavored dessert) and a Caesar salad (following the original recipe).

My idea, simple as it was, was to create an ambiance where the customer felt valued and taken care of while dining on the best meal in all of Houston. My customers are everything to me, I feel, and every customer would be welcomed as a part of my family.

The name of my restaurant would reflect the food and this spirit of the customers as family: *La Trattoria Ristorante Italiana*. A trattoria is a casual Italian eatery serving simple regional food with reasonable prices. Its linguistic roots are *trattare*, to treat, and *trattore*, an innkeeper or host. What name could better embody my restaurant?

Finally, the day arrived. The restaurant was ready, I had hired a staff, we had our menu set, and the kitchen was stocked. La Trattoria's grand opening and ribbon-cutting was set for November 6, 1983. Since my friend Greg Harbar had encouraged me to come to Houston, I arranged for The Gypsies to provide the music that day.

The mayor of Houston, Kathy Whitmire, sent a representative from her office to cut the ceremonial ribbon. One of the Houston newspapers published an article to announce the opening of my exciting new venture.

I was both excited and a little nervous. I had worked so many long years for this, driven all that time by my mama's faith and support for me. I stood in my restaurant's kitchen. It was a long journey for me from those early days in Italy to standing in my own place.

My thoughts turned to mama as the first customers came in. I recalled the little kitchen back in Cerea where I would help my mama prepare our simple yet delicious meals. I wished she were there, to stand beside me in the kitchen like the old days.

Our opening went well. We were very busy and the diners were all raving about the food and the service. We offered both lunch and dinner service Monday through

Saturday, closing all day on Sunday. Along with the dining area, the restaurant featured a small patio out front with a few tables for *al fresco* dining.

The restaurant was located along the very busy Westheimer Road with all its businesses and restaurants, just a short distance from the high-end shopping center The Galleria. I was going to have a lot of competition for diners, but I knew my approach to fresh, high-quality ingredients and simple dishes would win me customers.

I hired a maître d' to greet customers while I worked in the kitchen to prepare the food with the other back-of-house staff. However, I wanted customers to know me first and foremost, to know who was in the kitchen preparing their food with love. I put a bell on the door so I could hear when it opened. I got in the habit of looking out from the kitchen every time the bell on the front door jingled. I would come out to personally greet each new customer.

I always have loved birds, so I thought about taking a page from the Aldo restaurant's book back in Milan. Maybe I should get a parrot or cockatoo to chirp out a welcome in Italian to the customers. But then in dawned on me: no bird could handle that job better than I could. Plus, it might not have met the city's health code standards.

I set out to train my waiters to be very professional in every aspect of service, from the moment the customer sits down until he or she leaves. I wanted them to have an eagle eye, seeing everything that goes on and overlooking nothing. I impressed upon them that by doing this, they could anticipate customer needs and quickly meet them.

Also, I passed along some basic service tips and techniques. There is the proper way to carry a plate without touching the top surface with your fingers. You should serve from the left and clear from the right. Drape a napkin over your arm a few inches above your wrist, not hanging offensively from a belt or back pocket. There are so many easy, basic things to do to provide outstanding service to the diners.

Another important lesson I wanted to impart on my employees was to check on and around a table when the guests had left. We didn't want the guests to lose or leave behind anything of value. In the past, I had an incident that could have cost me a lot of money.

One day, a lady called the restaurant about half an hour after she had left. She was frantic, telling us she lost her engagement ring; she believed it was somewhere in the restaurant. "By any chance, have you found it?" she said, trying hard to remain calm.

I asked the waiter who had served her party if he had found it. He replied no. I decided to double check and walked over to the table. I found the ring stuck on the leg of the table! I told her we had the ring and would keep it safe until she returned.

Rushing into the restaurant, the lady embraced me with joy and kissed me on both cheeks. "This engagement ring is worth twenty-five thousand dollars!" she shouted. My eyes went wide. My guest was relieved and thrilled as she departed. I'm glad we had located it for her. The waiter had looked, just not thoroughly enough. The situation, which could have resulted in a black eye for the restaurant, turned out well.

Each time I tried to teach someone on my staff these essential lessons, I thought about my mama. "Son, when you do something, do it right and do it better than anybody." Recalling her words motivated me, infusing me with an incredible surge of energy that pushed me along the right path.

Speaking of family, my daughter Sofia Christina kept asking me if she could be a waitress at the restaurant. I would patiently and lovingly tell her no, that I wanted her to focus on her studies. I was determined she would get a better education than I did. We were sending her to a private Christian school and I wanted her to learn as much as she could without distraction.

I was having difficulties with the staff learning these lessons, but I was determined to press on, not give up. These are vital lessons, which play a key part in the success of a restaurant. I wanted to bring together the best of what I had learned through all my restaurant experiences. I had learned these skills over many years and wanted to pass them on to my staff.

Also, I found it difficult in those days to find quality food suppliers. I would drive thirty miles to Seabrook near the Galveston Bay waterfront to buy my fish. The market I shopped at reminded me of Aldo in Milan, where I could see for myself how fresh it was. Much of the fish was truly fresh off the boat as commercial fishing operations docked and offloaded catches directly from the Gulf of Mexico.

I bought most of my vegetables on my return trip, from an outdoor market called Canino Produce. They didn't carry the romaine lettuce that I needed for my Caesar salad, so I had to make a separate stop for that. I bought my baguettes from the best bakery in Houston at the time, El Hornito.

Most days, I would leave the house at six in the morning, visit all my stops to get the necessary supplies then race back to be in the kitchen by ten to start cooking. I lost track of the number of speeding tickets I got. One judge told me, "Carlo, slow down, you are not on an *autostrade* in Italy." These trips made my life difficult, but I was determined to procure the freshest ingredients for my dishes, no matter how much the traffic tickets cost me.

I would keep this up until I could find good-quality suppliers who would deliver to my door. Six months passed until I had located suppliers I could trust. I finally started to place my orders with them instead of burning up gas and time on the highways (oh, and paying those speeding fines).

I always emphasized top quality with my suppliers. Certain suppliers even told me, "Carlo, you are the only one in Houston that doesn't ask the price." I replied to them, "Well, I am more interested in getting top quality." They told me that most of their other customers drove them crazy asking about price.

These suppliers wanted to see the results of my drive for quality ingredients for themselves. They came in to try my food, quickly becoming some of my restaurant's best customers. For one thing, they knew first-hand how good the raw ingredients I used actually were. For another, this made for good business. Just like the relationship with my banker, we got to know each other.

With some patience, I tried to teach my waitstaff the art of tableside cooking. I spent a lot of time training them but didn't see much progress. Eventually, I was forced to give this up, except on special occasions. Then, I would step out of the kitchen and do it myself, putting on a show for my guests (and the hope was for my employees as well).

I faced difficulties with my kitchen staff as well. Some of them proved unreliable, in ways that baffled me. For many of the men whom I had worked beside in the kitchen over the years, they treated the positions in the kitchen as good, solid jobs and worked hard to exceed expectations. These were the kind of jobs that inspired me to leave my own country years earlier and past co-workers to leave theirs.

My goal was to teach my cooks to be master chefs, just as a young person might have learned in ages past to be a master craftsman or painter after serving an apprenticeship. "You have to learn to create a master dish," I explained to them.

"When you add ingredients to the dish, taste it over and over and think*: Is this what it's supposed to taste like?* Continue tasting until you are satisfied. Don't be afraid to fail. Then do it all over again." I had failed in the past and embraced those moments as opportunities to learn and improve.

I reminded my employees the reason why my customers came to the restaurant was because I was known for producing master dishes. If the dishes did not meet my standards, I would have to let the chef go.

However, if they could create such as dish, they would have proven themselves not only to me, but themselves. I would work hard to teach them skills and knowledge that would cost them thousands of dollars to learn at a traditional culinary school. I wanted them to learn. I was ready to teach them.

I also rewarded them when they did well, providing bottles of wine, cash, or other gifts to express my appreciation. This was my carrot-and-stick approach, I suppose. But I could think of no other way to describe the opportunity for learning that waited in my kitchen.

True, it was a high-pressure environment. There were pressures we were all under, night after night, to not let the customers down. To exceed expectations. It was nothing more, but nothing less, than I'd learned as a young man in Italy and other countries.

The chefs I hired didn't see it that way. I went through several of them, each time training them in true Italian cooking. Two chefs were Italian-American and one was from Sicily. I just couldn't get them to work with me and follow the methods I was teaching. When they would leave in frustration after several months, I was never sorry to see them go. I was determined to never compromise the style of my food.

I had exacting, but not unreasonable, standards. It was my restaurant that I had toiled so long for; I had a lofty vision and goals for La Trattoria. No compromise at all. I held my staff to the same quality expectations as I held for my ingredients.

Actually, the only staff member who seemed eager to please and work hard was not a chef but my enthusiastic prep cook from the state of Michoacán, Mexico.

Each time I bid farewell (and sometimes good riddance) to another chef, he pleaded for the opportunity to learn.

His name was Rafael Galvan. He was young, hardworking, and ambitious. I liked him. Perhaps he reminded me of myself when I was so eager to learn, learn more, and then learn even more than that. So about three and a half years after La Trattoria first opened, I decided he had earned a chance.

On Mother's Day 1986, I asked Galvan to stand beside me in the kitchen. I instructed him to watch, learn, and make my art and craft his own. "If you like this, you have to make a choice," I explained. "And if you choose this, do the very best you can, always, and you will be successful."

Within three years, he learned almost everything I could teach him. He was always ready to learn something new and tackle new challenges. I made sure to take care of him, paying him a very good salary, sharing the restaurant's profits, and offering paid vacation. I knew I had made the right choice. He remained by my side in that kitchen for twenty years.

I had someone to truly help me in the kitchen now. Everything was going well. Although the Houston economy had taken a downturn, I was building up a strong client base with many loyal customers. As restaurants around me failed, La Trattoria continued to do well. I often thought *do your best, and the money will follow*. Well, it was happening.

I received numerous write-ups in Houston magazines and newspapers and my food won some awards. The Zagat Houston Restaurant Survey recognized the restaurant as Excellent, "One of the Area's Finest Restaurants." And just as important, we were given high marks (a Blue Ribbon Award) in kitchen cleanliness by a local TV watchdog, Marvin Zindler.

Zindler, coincidentally, was made nationally famous by the movie *Best Little Whorehouse In Texas*. It was his investigative reporting on the La Grange, Texas, infamous Chicken Ranch that led to the exposure and closing of that storied establishment.

I did an interview with a local television station; another time, I was invited to give a cooking demonstration on TV. I presented another demonstration at a newly opened upscale grocery retailer from a large Texas-based chain. Word was getting out, and business picked up considerably.

La Trattoria's fame began to grow. The restaurant was a long-standing entry on one of the *Houston Chronicle* newspaper's list of favorite restaurants. "A perennial favorite for authentic, traditional Italian fare from chef-owner Carlo Molinaro. Charming, intimate setting; well-chosen, extensive Italian wine list. Simple yet wholly satisfying penne pasta coated with a lively three-pepper sauce and toothy spaghetti tossed with crispy, golden garlic and olive oil. Leave room for luscious homemade coffee-dipped tiramisu," the review stated.

Texas Monthly, a magazine dedicated to news, politics, culture, arts and cuisine from the Lone Star state, reviewed the restaurant by writing Chef Carlo's "attention to detail is evident in everything from the thoughtful presentation of the garlicky shrimp appetizer to the crisp greens in the house salad." The review added, "The lasagna, lauded as 'the best outside of Bologna,' was richly layered but light."

My frequent customers included wealthy residents in the community, politicians, and leaders from prominent local corporations from the energy and transportation industries, along with everyday Houstonians.

These customers came from all walks of life, many different cultures, and even spoke various languages. This is when respect and discipline paid dividends. I aimed to make everyone feel comfortable and at home in my place.

Studying all those languages during my career was a big help. I was often able to step out of the kitchen and take an order from guests speaking one of the languages of my life, not only Italian, German, or French, but also Sofia's Portuguese. This last language came in especially handy when the guests were from Brazil, often in town on oil business. I even had my menu translated into Japanese to accommodate a prominent Japanese firm with two thousand employees in Houston.

Many restaurants try to capitalize on the celebrity of their high-profile customers. I did not believe in that. When someone famous came into my restaurant, I wanted them to feel relaxed and welcome. I would never fawn all over celebrities. I forbid my staff from doing so, as well. They were told not to ask to take photos or get an autograph.

When a customer came to my restaurant, it was to enjoy our service and the best food we could provide. They deserved their privacy. I valued my customers as part of my family. I wanted my family to feel comfortable, without worrying about being in the limelight.

Admittedly, my public relations people over the years repeatedly begged me to approach my more famous guests about letting me "drop" their names to society columnists (they used to be called "gossip columnists" for a good reason). I was uncomfortable with that and I declined.

Since many years have passed and my restaurant is closed, I feel a little different about my previous policy. Now, I feel it's okay to talk about some of my more famous guests. A number of stars and musicians would dine at my place. Former Texas Governor Mark White followed me from The Palm to my new restaurant.

The restaurant's fame grew not just in Houston, but also around the country and even other parts of the world. Houston is truly an international city, with companies and governments from around the globe locating offices there. With so many of our guests coming from other countries, they told their fellow countrymen to try our food when they came to town.

I had a number of guests who were high-level political figures in Italy, such as the Prime Minister, the Consul, and my country's Ambassador to the United States. It was an honor for me, Italian born and raised, to host these people. I wanted them to experience a little bit of home while in the United States.

I even had a former President of the United States dine in my humble establishment. Yes, although I don't like to throw names around, one of the biggest honors paid to my restaurant was the visit of U.S. President George H.W. Bush.

He was very complimentary about the food and service. During one of several meals with us, he remarked, "Carlo, I don't know what you did, but I enjoyed broccoli for the first time in my life." This from the man who publicly denounced broccoli. I could not have been more proud.

Yet despite the fame and growing popularity of my restaurant, I insisted on limiting my dining room to the twelve tables. I had learned some techniques from top professionals on how to run a business in any situation, including making the most with little space.

A lesson I recalled from London showed me it doesn't matter how many tables you have. What really counts is how many customers you can serve in the space and time you have. Typically, I could serve fifty to seventy customers a night. I say with pride that on special occasions and holidays like Valentine's Day or New Year's Eve, we could serve up to 140. Considering we only had forty-eight seats, the accomplishment is amazing.

One technique I developed, which I played to the hilt quite successfully, was coming around as a party had finished dinner but were lingering. I would ask the group if they had enjoyed their dinner. "Oh yes," would come the enthusiastic reply. I would respond with, "Well, that's wonderful! I'd really love to buy you a drink or get you some dessert at the bar."

People tend not to turn down a free drink or dessert. They don't feel like they're being rushed from the table if treated to a simple act of friendship. The miniscule hard cost of a drink or dessert gave me access to the table where I could make more money.

I wanted to clear the table in a way that left the guests with good feelings, and a positive experience, unlike today when so many restaurants rush diners in and out like cattle. Pay and get out. These restaurants purposefully turn up the AC to make the room unpleasant so guests leave quickly. I can't stand these practices.

In summer 1988, the business next door to mine announced it was closing. This was an opportunity to expand I couldn't pass up. I didn't want to increase the space in the dining area and the number of tables. No, I had a different idea: I wanted to open a wine cellar for private parties and events.

I made an appointment with my banker. We spoke about my proposed expansion and hashed out the numbers. With funding secured, I contacted my landlord to negotiate. I proposed that they would rent the adjacent space to me for the same price per square foot as my current lease. They agreed and within two weeks we signed the papers.

I was on to my next venture. In the new space, I envisioned a room that would accommodate wine storage, an attractive dining area, and a wine bar. Harkening back to my days working at the Brückenkeller, I wanted to model my new project after the German restaurant's spacious wine cellar.

I met with a builder I knew and supplied him with a photo I had taken of Brückenkeller's cellar. Together we designed my wine cellar and I gave the builder the go-ahead. By the time it was completed, I had spent a quarter of a million dollars.

Although this was a lot of money, it was well spent. I was certain my contractor had built the most beautiful wine cellar in all of the United States. Everybody who came agreed, including the publication Wine Spectator, which deemed it one of the best wine cellars in the entire country.

Things were going well for my enterprises. Despite the continuing woes of Houston's oil-based economy, business was good enough that I was covering all my commitments. I felt very good about what I had created. But naturally, calm seas do not make good sailors.

Six months after I had invested so heavily into my new wine cellar, I would be severely impacted by a real estate debacle. My landlord defaulted on his debt; the entire property that was home to my restaurant and wine cellar went into foreclosure.

I was horrified. I had virtually no money left to fall back on, having plowed most of my cash reserves into opening the wine cellar. I felt panicked. What was going to happen? What could I do? I decided to approach the bank representatives about the foreclosure. I suggested they work with me to find a way for me to purchase the property. They would not consider my proposal.

Despite my business success, I guess they considered my potential venture into real estate too risky. Shortly after that a real estate company, a client of the bank, bought the property instead. I anxiously wondered what impact this would have on me. I found out soon enough and it wasn't good.

A few weeks after the sale, my new landlord sent me a registered letter terminating my lease. I was presented with two choices, the letter stated: 1) I could agree to pay double my current rent, or 2) I could vacate the property in four weeks. I was stunned. I could not believe what was happening to my American Dream.

Essentially, I felt like I was being held hostage. I was between the proverbial rock and a hard place. The situation looked dire. I headed straight to the real estate office to explain that I had just invested a quarter of a million dollars to improve the property.

Surely my expenditures counted for something, I told an agent. Doubling my rent on top of my huge outlay would be excessive. The agent shrugged. This was business, he insisted. I could agree to the increase or leave.

I wanted to scream at the unfairness of the situation. I had little choice. I could either walk away, essentially giving the landlord a gift of a quarter-million dollars or agree to double my current rent. How could this happen. How could the company get away with this?

Well, all is fair in love, politics, and real estate. So, I caved and in the end did what anyone faced with this complicated position would do. I signed the new lease and agreed to pay the higher monthly rent. My hope was that I could earn enough, even in such a tough economy. I now had to cover both the rent increase and the monthly debt payment for the improvements, along with my usual operating expenses.

Once again, I was learning lessons the hard way. I was in the restaurant business, which I could handle, but now I was schooled on real estate markets and economics. The real estate company had won, for now. I would eventually turn the tables, but for now I reluctantly paid the higher rent.

Fortunately for me, I was able to stay above water while the slumping Houston economy slowly pulled out of its nosedive. I didn't have to cut any corners to make ends meet. It's just as well; I would never have compromised on anything, either quality or service.

Business picked up considerably. It was going so well that by 1992, I not only covered my costs, I was turning a tidy profit. I earned enough to replenish my depleted cash reserves. I decided it was time for me to take the next step in my career.

In Italy, we say, *"Trovarsi fra l'incudine e il Mmartello,"* when we are in a bad situation. The phrase means to be between the anvil and the hammer. Well, I did not want to be placed between the anvil and hammer anymore when it came to real estate dealings. I wanted to be the blacksmith, so to speak, in charge of my own destiny.

I put together a package of paperwork and approached my bank about a loan to buy the building. I wanted to be my own landlord. I met with a loan officer and we discussed my loan papers and all my business records. I left the meeting knowing I had done everything I could to make my case.

The bank reviewed the paperwork then agreed that I could manage it. It would be a good investment. I was ready to approach my landlord next. I intended to, as Vito Corleone would say, "make them an offer they could not refuse."

Well, it turns out I didn't have to carry my Godfather approach out after all. Without too much unpleasantness, my landlord saw the good sense in selling the building to me. We completed the deal, and the building was finally mine. I was not only a restaurant owner now, but a budding real estate mogul! No more unexpected rent hikes; I had moved out from between the anvil and hammer.

I had a budding little empire at this point. In addition to La Trattoria, I had the wine cellar for private parties and the wine bar. Adjacent to that space, I had opened a small wine bar not only to serve a fine selection of wines, but also to introduce Americans to another cultural practice in Europe. The bar would serve tapas, as they are called in Spanish, but known here as "small plates."

This was a relatively new concept to the Houston culinary scene. These small plates were like individual hot or cold appetizers, not a full entrée. The intent was to have something to nibble on while guests drink their wine. Because the portion size was reduced, you could order a variety of items and not fill up. Patrons could try a selection of meats, cheeses, or vegetables to pair with their wine selection.

Unfortunately, I think this idea was ahead of its time. Soon it became clear to me that people came to my restaurant to dine, not nibble. With a touch of regret— since I myself enjoy having a few bites with a glass of wine— I closed the wine bar. Friends and guests suggested to me that Americans were not ready for a wine bar and small plates. Now, they are very popular. Often, timing is everything.

Despite the disappointment, we gained a reputation for having one of the best wine lists around. My passion for wine, kindled and nurtured all those years ago in Italy, was paying off. Like my search for the highest-quality ingredients for our dishes, I sought out the best wines for my cellar and to serve with our food. I had been very interested in learning about wine for a long time.

Once again, my thirst (pardon the pun) for knowledge motivated me to learn more about the history of wine, how it is made, and all the endless grape varietals, wine regions, and wine-making styles. I channeled this interest in various ways.

In 1985, I started going to my native Verona's VinItaly each year, the largest wine exhibition in the world. I would rub elbows and clink glasses with the likes of Italian winemakers from Antinori, Bertani, Gaia, and Frescobaldi.

Just as importantly, I met with all the best import companies. They understood the challenges and intricacies of navigating the U.S. and Texas alcohol import laws, so I could obtain wines from outside America and pour them at my restaurant.

All this effort translated into a world-class collection. The *Wine Spectator* wrote an article featuring our wines, bringing attention to it. We received an Award of Excellence for "having one of the most outstanding restaurant wine lists in the world."

We stocked a total of four hundred and fifty different types of wines, around ten thousand total bottles. Our selections spanned Italian, California, and French wines, dating as far back as 1945. This year always gave me a secret sense of satisfaction, since it marked the end of the terrible war that had shaped my childhood. This year also marked the beginning of the modern age for European, and especially French, wines.

The grand old houses of Bordeaux, Burgundy, and even Champagne could return to making some of the best wines on earth, following the liberation of France by Allied forces and the end of World War II. They were free again to produce their fine beverages and distribute them around the world, no longing fearing their handiwork would be guzzled by the loutish Nazi overlords. So yes, 1945 *was* a good year in my mind.

I purchased a purebred boxer puppy in 1994. It was the first animal I could truly say was my pet. I named him Tyson, because he was a boxer. Too clever, eh? I had him for 12 years. We arranged a girlfriend for him, Maya, so they could have a litter of puppies. When they first met, it was almost like they embraced. It was true puppy love. She had three puppies. I keep saying one day I will get another dog, but it hasn't happened yet.

Anyway, back to the restaurant. Our simple, fresh dishes, renowned customer service, and sterling reputation had attracted attention from other restaurant-oriented businesses. In early 2000, I was approached by a New York company with an offer to franchise my restaurant.

A representative contacted me with what he indicated was a lucrative offer if I agreed to a franchising opportunity for La Trattoria. I was skeptical but willing to listen. They proposed a fee of fifty thousand dollars to me if I provided three to four months of training for potential franchisees. In addition, once each franchised eatery opened, I would receive 3.5 to 4.5 percent of the gross revenue.

This affirmed to me that I was doing things the right way to attract this kind of attention. I pondered the offer. I admit, the idea of teaching others my style and approach to Italian cuisine was tempting. *But could I really teach someone to cook the way I did in just three or four months?* I had taken nearly thirty years to learn and master my techniques and skills. And what if I didn't like the food produced by their chefs and cooks? Or what if they didn't want to learn?

I already had enough trouble with my own kitchen staff. I was very exacting about what happened in my own place. I realized I wouldn't have a lot of say in the matter. The franchises would all be on their own after my initial training.

I considered what I had built and worked so hard for over the last three decades. My name and my reputation meant something. I did all this for my mama, Olga Molinaro. Her name meant something to me. What if the franchises weren't as devoted to protecting my name and reputation as I was? Was it realistic to even expect this?

I thought long and hard about the pros and cons. In the end, there were too many factors out of my control. Plus, I knew I was not willing to compromise my name and reputation. Those were everything to me. In one sense, my name was the only true thing I had carried with me from those days in Cerea and Sanguinetto.

So as much as the offer intrigued me, I turned it down. I walked away from the money and potential fame to keep my name and reputation. There is no price on that. Since that time, many other Italian restaurants have grown nationwide through franchising and other business models since then. You just have to drive through any suburban strip mall to see them. However, I have never, ever regretted my decision.

Three years later, in 2003, La Trattoria celebrated a true milestone. We had been in business for twenty years. The restaurant business is tough. So many factors are out of your control: rent, food and transportation costs, finding good staff, competition, the economy, and so on. Between twenty and twenty-five percent of restaurants do not survive their first year of operation. And here we were at twenty years.

This was an amazing feat, truly a reason to celebrate. I wanted to say thank you to all my customers, so I invited them to a party. Boy, did they show up. They filled the dining room, the bar, and the wine room, and they even spilled out onto the patio that looked out through vines to the 24/7 traffic of Westheimer.

We all ate and drank together, one big sea of happy faces, into the early hours of the morning. And because a party isn't a party without great music, we all listened, danced, and sang along to the fabulous The Gypsies. We partied well into the night. It was quite the affair.

La Trattoria would reach another milestone, twenty-five years, before my own personal situation would take a turn for the worse. Sometimes, especially as a person gets older, health issues end up having as much to do with running a business as typical business issues do. This fact become especially clear (and painful) when that person operates the business on his own, with limited help from employees.

My health issues started in the spring of 2001. I had visited my doctor for a routine physical examination. The doctor told me, "You have a hernia that's not getting any better." Well, that was not what I expected to hear. "What does this mean?" I asked. "You need surgery to repair it," he stated.

Following the surgery, I would need to stay home and recuperate for at least six days, the doctor cautioned me. This meant I would need to close the restaurant for nearly a week. I underwent the surgery and began my recovery. After a couple of days, my strength had improved and I felt better. I decided to reopen the restaurant ahead of schedule.

A couple of days later, I was doing much better and didn't seem to be suffering any after-effects of the surgery. I drove home after closing, stopping my car in the driveway while I opened the garage door. The remote control had fallen to the floor of the car. With the car idling in the drive, I fished around for the remote.

Suddenly, my foot slipped off the brake and the car lurched forward towards the still-closed door. Frantically, I pressed hard on what I thought was the brake. Instead, it was the accelerator. The car crashed through the garage door before I could stop it.

I got out of the car to inspect the damage, upset with myself. The spring plate from the door was wedged beneath the car's front wheel. I wondered what to do next, uncertain on how to proceed. As I looked at the damage, the unthinkable happened. The powerful spring, under tension, broke free and shot straight for me!

I couldn't get out of the way, and the metal object struck me hard on the right side of the head. I was knocked to the ground. Dazed, I lay on the ground bleeding. Sofia had heard the commotion and come out to check on me. She immediately rushed me to the emergency room.

"Were you in a fight?" the ER doctor asked; he didn't seem to be making a joke. "You could say that," I said "I accidentally drove through the garage door. It fought back. It won." I explained, still stunned about what had happened. The diagnosis: my right eye and ear were severely injured.

He handed me a prescription for eye drops. "Use these and you should be better in a week." Two weeks later, I was still suffering. I followed up my regular eye doctor. He examined me, saying "Your eye is infected." He then admonished me. "Why did you leave it this long?"

I explained what had happened, adding I had no idea my eye was infected. "If you were a young man, it would probably recover, at least reasonably so." He continued "But you're not twenty, you're fifty. At fifty, you just don't heal as fast or as well."

I was having an ongoing problem with my ear, also. I consulted with an ear specialist. He presented me with two options: medication or surgery. I didn't want to undergo more surgery, not after the hernia operation. I would have to close the restaurant again. I chose the medication option.

I ended up losing part of the sight in my right eye and much of the hearing in my right ear. (Now if anyone ever needs to sneak up on me, approach from the right.) With my reduced vision and hearing, this would significantly impact my ability to keep up with the restaurant.

I was persistent and stubborn, so I vowed not to let my disabilities hinder my work. I trudged on until a year later, when I was diagnosed with an enlarged prostate. After my initial appointment, three weeks passed with no update on my condition from my doctor. I decided to see another physician, who was a regular customer at La Trattoria.

I figured this doctor would be motivated to treat me and get me back to cooking in the restaurant. It wasn't serious, the doctor told me. I was relieved. "It's nothing more than an irritation," he reassured me. "I'll prescribe you some medication. But what I really want you to do is relax and have a glass of red wine in the evening occasionally." I could handle drinking a glass of wine, on doctor's orders. "You're too stressed out, Carlo. That's the real problem."

How to relax, though? I've been working for around fifty years. I have been driven during that time to work hard and keep learning as much as I could. Relaxation was difficult for me. To make matters worse, I was about to receive more bad news.

It was about this time that Rafael, the prep cook I had trained to function as my assistant chef so many years earlier, turned in his notice. He wanted to open his own restaurant. I couldn't blame him, but I was sorry to see him go. The kitchen would be short-handed and I wasn't one hundred percent.

Week after week, I struggled to find a viable candidate to replace Rafael. But times were changing in my industry, faster than I could keep up. Many restaurants were trying experimental concepts and implementing "fusion" cuisine, combining two different types to create all new dishes.

I don't think there were two or more cuisines on earth that hadn't been fused together. Before this trend faded into something more like good sense, I am sure there were many disastrous dishes. I'm glad I missed tasting most of them. I called this style more "confusion" than anything. Why be a Picasso, in my opinion, when you could me a Michelangelo?

This is when the chef as a personality, larger than life, began to develop. Chefs were becoming stars. It was more about the style than the substance. Many of them made a name for themselves by putting out the wildest and weirdest dishes I could imagine.

I brought in quite a few cooks to "audition" during this drawn-out and difficult period. Some came with impressive resumes. The issue was they all thought they knew everything already. Nobody wanted to learn anything. Those that thought they knew Italian were more familiar with the Italian-American style of cooking than the regional cuisine found back home in Italy.

The many nights I spent with these cooks in the kitchen felt hopeless. I worked myself to death trying to keep my regular guests from noticing. The minute I was out in the dining room to greet our customers, the chef would revert to some pop version of vaguely Italian fast food. A few guests knew how difficult the situation was and they were sympathetic and encouraging.

I was feeling very discouraged, though. I really needed to find someone like Rafael but it wasn't happening. I felt like I couldn't leave the kitchen, yet I wanted to get out and interact with my customers. As bad as things were, they were about to get worse.

Along with the right side of my face and my prostate giving me trouble, my right shoulder joined the party, too. Two different doctors recommended surgery to repair my rotator cuff. I listened in disbelief when they said this would require me to stay home and recover for six months. *Six months?* I could barely handle closing the restaurant for less than a week. There was no way I could turn over the restaurant operations or trust the kitchen duties to anyone else.

I hesitated to undergo surgery, as I was reluctant to close my restaurant for that long. Any decision, however, was taken out of my hands. Nature was about to play a part in all this now. A Category 2 hurricane, Ike, struck the Gulf Coast at Galveston, south of Houston. High winds and rain from the severe storm pummeled the area, resulting in major damage to my business and building.

At the time, the hurricane caused the third worst amount in damages in U.S. history. For two weeks, the water and electricity were cut off to the building. I had no choice but to close the restaurant while the repairs were made. To rub salt in the wound, after the disaster was over I received very little insurance settlement. The premises had suffered over forty thousand dollars in damage and I received less than a quarter of that from my insurance company.

After the storm passed and the utilities were restored, we made the necessary repairs to the restaurant and we reopened. During the time off, I was able to get some rest and my health improved some. Despite the restaurant being back up and running, dark clouds continued to loom over me. To complicate matters, Sofia and I decided to divorce. We had grown apart through the years, as happens sometimes, and there was no reason for us to stay married.

Our daughter Sofia Cristina was now living in the Los Angeles area. When she was growing up, I was determined to provide her with schooling opportunities that my father had taken away from me. I wanted her to attend good schools and get a quality education.

We had sent her to private schools in Houston, and she had earned bachelor's and master's degrees at universities in California. She achieved something I was deprived the opportunity to do.

She married and in 2006, gave birth to my first grandchild, Ella. After a career in education, Sofia now runs a successful jewelry design business in Santa Monica, California. I'm very proud of all that she has accomplished, especially owning her own company.

I had reached a point where I had to make a decision about the restaurant. I understood that work, stressful enough on the best of days, was more than my current health could handle. I wanted to go out on top, though, before my health prevented me from continuing. The decision was difficult and sad, but I didn't feel I had any other options. I was going to close my restaurant permanently.

My special recipe for you: Penne ai Tre Pepperoni (Three Peppers)

This was always one of my customers' favorite pastas, and certainly a dish I love to make for friends now that I am retired. It is one of my daughter's favorites, too.

The sweetness delivered to this sauce by the lightly caramelized bell peppers and onion is a joy to behold.

Serving size: 4

Ingredients:

1 red bell pepper

1 green bell pepper

1 yellow bell pepper

1 yellow onion

1 cup extra-virgin olive oil

1 8-oz can crushed tomatoes

Salt and pepper to taste

1 tablespoon butter

4 cups cooked penne

Grated Parmigiano Reggiano

Directions:

1. Dice the peppers and onions.
2. Cook the penne pasta according to the package directions.
3. Over medium-low heat, cook the peppers and onion in the olive oil until they start to turn soft.
4. Add the crushed tomatoes and cook for about 10 to 15 minutes.
5. Season the sauce with salt and pepper to taste.
6. Add the butter, stirring gently.
7. Once the butter is incorporated, remove the sauce from the heat.
8. Pass this sauce mixture through a vegetable strainer.
9. Toss the sauce and penne in the pot until thoroughly mixed.
10. Serve with grated Parmigiana.

Chapter 12: *Lezioni Apprese*

Lessons Learned

I really wasn't ready to turn off the lights and shutter La Trattoria, but I felt strongly about going out on my own terms. I wanted to go out on top. Like a pro soccer star or top tennis player who just won a championship and announced his or her retirement while hoisting the trophy.

I wracked my brain for ways to keep the restaurant going, at least to make it through to celebrate three decades. But I was out of ideas. My health, combined with a never-ending search for good staff (especially kitchen staff), sealed my decision and the restaurant's fate. I informed my guests of the decision and broke the news to my staff.

My only consolation to my decision was the thought that I might try again someday. I could take a little time off to rest and recuperate, maybe get the surgery and treatment my poor body needed. Then maybe I could open a smaller version of La Trattoria, keeping it simple. I knew how to do simple; that could work.

Or maybe I'd channel my love for wine into another Italian wine bar, with a limited food menu but a treasure trove of Italian wines. I could spend more time with my customers, regaling them with tall tales from my life. I daydreamed about this scenario and how much I would enjoy such a life, since I always enjoyed interaction with my customers.

Those potential plans were in the future and I put those thoughts aside. I had a big party to plan at the restaurant. I wanted this to be the biggest and best party my customers had ever attended. I wanted to celebrate what I had accomplished for twenty-eight years with La Trattoria and even longer in the restaurant business, not mourn what I was being forced to give up.

I invited all my longtime customers, who I now considered to be friends, even family. I felt genuine feelings for all of them, knowing that over the years they came to visit me at the restaurant more than just to spend money and eat a fine meal.

I planned an over-the-top amount of food. We had prepped and cooked for the party for three days. We wanted everyone to have enough food. We didn't care if we ran out of everything. I arranged for my friend Greg Harbar and The Gypsies to perform. We were going to mark the closing in style. The party was set for December 18, 2010, exactly nine months before my seventieth birthday.

The final day came around and the restaurant was packed with around two hundred guests. The food for the party was all Italian classics. It was exactly the food that my customers had come to count on from my kitchen, no matter how many new, modern, or creative touches rocked the Italian cuisine boat at other restaurants.

I wasn't especially interested in this fast-changing notion of good food, the trends that rose and faded in the food world. My food was grounded in what had always been good and, if you ask me, would always be good. Simple, fresh, and tasty. It was hard to improve upon this basic approach.

My longtime customers agreed, which I guess explains why they stayed loyal over those many years. People I had known for nearly all my years in Houston passed plates around, sampling lasagna, spaghetti, osso buco, and veal parmigiana and piccata.

I looked around the restaurant time and again, not just at the surroundings and the financial position my decades of work had made possible, but mainly at the wealth of people surrounding me. These people were my second family that I had been happily feeding all these years.

Not bad for someone who was only allowed to attend school through the second grade, I thought. I smiled as I began to feel the warmth of the wine transform me, as it does so well. Many people stopped to say their goodbyes as the party began to wind down.

I made sure that anyone who told me they would miss my lasagna, tiramisu, or cassata took some home with them to enjoy the next day. It wouldn't last them forever, of course, but it was a small way of showing my gratitude for their loyalty.

"Carlo, we'll miss you," customer after customer came up to me to say, especially after all the wine took effect and the group was whittled down to just a few really close friends. The stalwarts had gathered around me outside on the patio, sitting and talking into the wee hours of the morning.

"It's a little like a funeral," someone said. I didn't feel that way. Yes, the party was quieting down, but no, it was always a celebration of the good and not a lamentation of the approaching end. It was an emotional farewell. I was touched, sad that it was all coming to an end.

Yet deep down, I remembered: *it is the right time.* It's better to retire when you are at the peak than tumble down the slope. Go out strong rather than linger on until you become weaker and your performance starts to decline. I wanted people to fondly recall me at my best.

The members of The Gypsies, the musical group so intertwined with me and my restaurant, sat with me long after the party ended. We reminisced about the lives we'd led and the faces we now missed. A lot had happened over the twenty-eight-year span of the restaurant.

Of course, I thought about my mama. I wished she had lived to see it all. She had started me on this journey of over sixty years with her belief in me and some down-to-earth advice. "Son, when you do something, do it better than anybody else," I heard her voice tell me once again. "Show respect and discipline yourself to learn, to always learn. There is no excuse for not doing your best."

The more I thought about her, the more I came to realize that she was the best teacher I ever had. She never sat me down and said, "Learn this," but she had a way of teaching me simple lessons about everyday life and how to succeed. I took her lessons to heart and faced every challenge that life had thrown at me.

I had never stopped learning. I had never stopped trying. I thought back to that little boy who struggled to make perfect furniture, learning from his mistakes. The teenage Carlo who learned how to clear tables and saw first-hand what outstanding service meant.

On to the eager young man who traveled to new countries, learning new languages and cultures, to better himself. How he watched other waiters and learned the proper way to wait on customers. He was persistent and always worked his way up, always remembering the importance of respect and discipline.

I recalled the younger me who'd lost his savings more than once but never let that deter his efforts to learn. Perseverance wouldn't let anything get in the way of that young man finding the next opportunity, greeting the next customer, learning the next lesson, and moving up the career path.

Next, I thought of the chefs who had willingly passed on their skills to me. They were pleased that I shared their passion for food. Some of my fondest memories of learning to cook involved me bringing a little wine or shared tip money to the chef in exchange for a lesson, recipe, or techniques.

My entire journey had led me to the opening of my restaurant. Now, on the verge of closing my beloved restaurant, what was next? This was a very bittersweet moment for me. The restaurant and I had been through so much together: joys and sorrows, challenges and triumphs, and undeniably, so many different employees.

Another thought popped into my head. Even though I was sad to let go of La Trattoria, to let go of what my life had become, I was so pleased and happy about all the years I had spent in my adopted country; I had the freedom to focus on finding success and achieving the goal I shared in my new home with so many other immigrants before me: the American dream.

There was plenty to be proud of in that achievement. It was the same pride I had tried to instill in each and every employee over the decades, some with greater success than others. Simply, I felt, that if I could work hard to attain my dream then they could too. I wanted others to share in this with me: a few would, some couldn't, while others simply wouldn't.

Well, all that battle was behind me now. The restaurant was now officially closed. Maybe I could finally get some rest now. Could I possibly find some peace and solace among all the accomplishments I had achieved, or would I still be motivated to do more?

Maybe I could...Stop! I ordered myself. There would be plenty of time tomorrow and in the following days to think such thoughts. For now, I just wanted to savor the moment. To drink in everything around me in these fading minutes of the night.

It was my finale as the owner and chef of La Trattoria. The curtain had closed and the lights were shut off. I was warmed by the wine, sitting contently on the patio, surround by the smiling faces of my friends and family.

I was so thankful for everything I had. My family. My success. My knowledge and skills. My opportunities. My experiences. Grazie, mama. For now, my hunger was sated.

That was eight years ago. The notion I had entertained of opening a smaller place or a wine bar did not happen. I decided to travel some, to relax and unwind for a while. I returned to Italy and other European locations, seeking out the places from my past. Most had changed, a few remained frozen in time.

It was a strange and wonderful trip. I visited family, took in familiar sights, tasted the food that had inspired me, drank wine, and even saw some familiar faces from my past (or relatives of those faces).

Back home in America, I pondered all I had seen and done on my trip. It started me thinking about what I wanted to do next. I was restless. I certainly wasn't ready to join a bridge club or play golf all the time.

Well, they say everyone has at least one book in them, so I decided it was time to write my story. I felt like I wanted to share what I had been through with others. For a boy who experienced war, never made it past the second grade, and who was always hungry, I had worked hard and achieved success. If I can do it, anyone can.

Writing this book has been a long, drawn out process, but Rome wasn't built in a day, right? I wanted to capture the simple principles that guided me on my journey. I reflected on what I had learned, the education I had made for myself. I boiled the essence of my self-taught lessons down to some key points.

1. Be respectful and practice discipline

This was the most important lesson in my life, the one my mama had taught me at a young age. If you show respect for others, you will go a long way. You should respect yourself, as well. By doing both, you can accomplish a lot.

Discipline is crucial. If you can remain disciplined throughout your life, no matter the situation, you can tackle the toughest challenges and face the unknown with a steadfast bearing. The two together are powerful tools that can guide you through both thick and thin.

2. Always do your best

This is another great lesson from my mama. Why do something if you aren't going to give it your all? When you decide to make an effort, put everything you have into it.

These days, it seems that people give a task a half-hearted attempted then say, "Good enough." I say no, *not* good enough. Go all in. Set a standard for yourself and maintain it, even if everyone around you isn't trying their hardest. It will set you apart.

3. Keep it simple

Why complicate things? When you cook, don't use a lot of ingredients. This just creates a messy dish with muddled flavors. In life, keep it simple. Complications create stress and that affects your health. Appreciate the simple things and you can bring balance to your life.

Crank up your favorite song as you're driving around and sing along. Take a nice walk with a loved one. Learn something new. Sip a nice glass of wine (or your beverage of choice). Enjoy a nice dessert or treat. Be thankful for the family and friends around you.

4. Be persistent

I always remain persistent, no matter what I face in life. Set a course and work toward it, no matter what looms before you. There were so many points in my life I could have given up, thrown up my hands and surrendered. Plenty of people around me did.

Did I give up when I lost large sums of money on different occasions? No. Did I give up when I was yanked out of school to get a job as a child? No. Did I give up when my mama died? No.

I had a goal and worked hard to reach it. At any point, it would have been much easier to quit than press on. But I never did. I had that star to guide me, my mama. Find your star to navigate you through life.

5. Believe in yourself and keep the faith

Like I said, find your star. Something that motivates you, challenges you, keeps you moving when there's no other reason. My mama believed in me. She told me she saw great things for me, despite my early age.

Her love and support started me on my journey and kept me on the path until I reached my goal. Your guiding star can be someone or something within you. Whatever that star is for you, hold fast to it. Even in the darkest times, remember it is still there. Just remind yourself of that.

6. Learn all the time

Education is so important. Seek it out. Whether it's school or life, there are lessons to be learned. You have to continuously seek out knowledge. What you learn can help you be successful, maybe not today but certainly at some point in your life.

There are no excuses. If I only finished second grade and still managed to succeed, you can too. Anyone can. You just have to want to learn. Hunger for it. You will find boundless opportunities to gain knowledge or skills when you decide to learn.

7. Do a good job and the money will follow

This is simple. Do your best all the time and you will be rewarded. You may not be rewarded right away, but you will be. You may have to find the right situation for you first, though. You may have to learn new skills and gain knowledge.

Work hard and remain persistent. Stay on track and follow your star. The money will come. It worked for me, there's no reason these simple rules won't work for you.

Thank you for joining me on my journey from wartime Italy to dreams in America. I would wish you, my dear reader, good luck. However, we don't necessarily say that in Italy. We say, "*In bocca al lupo,*" which means in the mouth of the wolf. Yes, it means good luck, in a way. It means go directly into your troubles. The response when someone tells you this? "*Crepi il lupo.*" May the wolf die.

I will leave you with one final thought, my friend: *Rimanere affamati per la vita.* Stay hungry for life.

My special recipe for you: Tiramisu

I figured this would be a sweet ending to this book.

This favorite dessert certainly made some waves when it started appearing on Italian (and even non-Italian) menus in the United States.

The name means "pick me up," a reference to the espresso, which can have that desired effect on almost anybody.

Serving size: 12

Ingredients

8 ounces mascarpone

1 cup powdered sugar

1 cup rum

4 eggs

1 egg white

60 ladyfingers

2 cups strong espresso

½ cup finely grated chocolate

Directions:

1. Using a blender or mixer, mix the mascarpone with the sugar, rum, eggs, and egg white until it forms a thick cream.

2. Spread about 2 tablespoons of the mascarpone mixture across the bottom of a 12 X 8-inch baking dish.

3. Dip each lady finger in the espresso and lay them across the mixture on the bottom of the dish.

4. Adding another layer of espresso-dipped lady fingers.

5. Spread another 2 tablespoons of the mascarpone mixture on the lady fingers layer (the middle of the dish).

6. Add another layer of lady fingers.

7. Pour the remainder of the mascarpone cream mixture on the top of the lady finger layers.

8. Top the with grated chocolate.

9. Refrigerate for at least 24 hours before serving.

Ricette preferite: Favorite Recipes

La Cucina Italiana L'arte di Mangiare Bene: Italian Cuisine is the Art of Good Eating

I've gathered some of my favorite recipes from over the years for you, all of which were on the menu at my restaurant, La Trattoria, at various times—including the simple broccoli dish President George H.W. Bush told me he really enjoyed.

When you're making these recipes, you should always taste the food and adjust any seasonings. It's better to under-season a dish and add to it while cooking than over-season it. And, you should always check your dishes carefully for doneness.

A simple secret for being a good cook is knowing when a dish is done and not overcooking or undercooking it. Always keep an eye on your food while cooking; with enough experience, you will gain a feel for when your dish is ready.

Fettucine alla Bolognese

As I learned from my earliest days in the restaurant business, you can't open anything devoted to Italian cuisine without some type of the dish on the menu called "Bolognese."

I think it's funny that the only place you can't order Bolognese is Bologna. There, this meat sauce is known simply as ragu.

Serving size: 6

Ingredients:

2 carrots

2 onions

2 celery stalks

¼ cup extra-virgin olive oil

¾ pound ground beef

½ pound ground veal

¼ pound ground pork

1 cup red wine

1 cup crushed tomatoes

2 tablespoons chopped parsley

2 tablespoons butter

Salt and pepper to taste

6 cups cooked fettuccine

Directions:

1. Finely chop the carrots, onion, and parsley.
2. Lightly caramelize the onion and carrots in the olive oil over medium heat.
3. Add the three types of meats and cook until almost done.

4. Add the red wine and stir until it evaporates.
5. Add the tomatoes and chopped celery, then reduce the heat and simmer for 1 hour.
6. Season with salt and pepper; stir in the parsley and butter.
7. The sauce is best if it cools off for about 12 hours for flavors to combine and intensify.
8. Reheat the sauce and toss with fettuccine until heated through.

Risotto Milanese

Of course, Italy is the home of pasta. There are hundreds of shapes and styles known by different names, even from village to village in the same valley of the same mountains.

Yet the great cooks of Milan gave the world a delicious alternative, made with the short-grain rice that's grown in a few sections of northern Italy.

Behold: risotto in the style of Milan.

Serving size: 4

Ingredients:

½ cup yellow onion

¼ cup extra-virgin olive oil

2 cups Arborio rice (any short, thick-grain rice can be used)

½ cup white wine

3 cups chicken broth

½ oz. Spanish saffron threads

Directions:

1. Dice the onion.
2. In a pot, lightly caramelize the onion in the olive oil over medium heat.
3. Add the rice and stir until it starts to look dry.
4. Add the wine and cook until nearly all the liquid is evaporated.
5. Add the saffron to the broth and add some broth to the rice; cook until the liquid is absorbed.
6. Keep adding broth in small amounts until the rice is cooked, about 20 to 25 minutes.
7. Serve either as an appetizer or a side dish.

Coniglio alla Cacciatora

This dish is similar to the popular chicken cacciatore, except the real name in Italian is never about the hunter (cacciatore) but about the hunter's wife (cacciatora). I feel it's time to correct the error perpetrated by Italian restaurants everywhere.

This dish uses rabbit, which I believe has more flavor than chicken anyway.

Serving size: 4-6

Ingredients:

½ cup yellow onions

½ cup extra-virgin olive oil

¾ cup canned crushed tomatoes

2 pounds fresh rabbit, prepared (cleaned with the head removed)

All-purpose flour seasoned with salt and pepper (enough to dredge the rabbit in)

1 cup white wine

10 oz. package sliced fresh mushrooms (white are best)

Salt and pepper to taste

1 cup chicken broth

1 tablespoon butter

1 tablespoon parsley

Cooked polenta (see the recipe in Chapter 1)

Directions:

1. Slice the onions and chop the parsley.
2. Cut the rabbit into serving pieces (remove the legs and cut 1- inch-long pieces along the body, leaving the bones in).
3. Lightly caramelize the onion in the olive oil, then add the crushed chopped tomatoes and simmer for 3 to 4 minutes.
4. Lightly coat the rabbit pieces in the seasoned flour and add them to the skillet, pressing down into the sauce mixture.
5. Cook for 5 minutes, then add the wine and cook for 5 minutes more.
6. Add the mushrooms and season the dish with salt and pepper to taste.

7. Add the chicken broth, butter, and parsley and cook until the rabbit is tender, about 5 minutes. (Flip the rabbit several times to cook it evenly; make sure sauce doesn't dry out; add the broth a little at a time while cooking.)

8. Serve hot over mounds of polenta (see the recipe in Chapter 1).

Veal Scaloppini al Limone

This is one of the most popular dishes credited to Milan. People love it because it's so light and fresh-tasting, with a simple sauce of lemon, butter, and a dry white wine.

Remember, don't ever cook with a wine you wouldn't be happy to drink!

Serving size: 2

Ingredients:

2 tablespoons extra-virgin olive oil

1 tablespoon butter (plus 1 tablespoon butter reserved)

1 cup all-purpose flour, seasoned with salt and pepper

6 thin slices veal, pounded out

½ cup white wine

Salt and pepper

Juice of ½ lemon

½ tablespoon freshly chopped parsley

Directions:

1. Heat the oil and 1 tablespoon butter in a pan over medium heat.
2. Dredge the veal in the seasoned flour and shake off the excess, then cook it briefly in the pan for about 30 seconds, turning once.
3. Melt the remaining tablespoon of butter in a separate pan.
4. Add the veal and the wine to the melted butter, cooking for less than a minute.
5. Season with salt and pepper.
6. Add the lemon juice and parsley.

Mozzarella in Carrozza

So many people think fried mozzarella comes in long sticks covered in thick breading. This fried mozzarella recipe, called mozzarella in a carriage, is such a simple dish to prepare.

It requires only a few ingredients and is ready in no time at all. It's very satisfying and makes a great appetizer. You can serve it with a fresh marinara sauce.

Serving size: 2

Ingredients:

8 slices white bread (thin)

8 oz. fresh mozzarella (preferably in a log form)

2 eggs

¼ cup half and half cream

Flour

Salt/pepper

Extra-virgin olive oil/vegetable oil mix (enough to cover the mozzarella when placed in the pan)

Directions:

1. Slice the mozzarella into pieces about 1/4 inch thick.
2. Place a slice of mozzarella in the middle of a slice of bread, then place another slice on top.
3. Use a biscuit cutter to cut away the bread crust or a knife to trim the bread; leave enough bread to crimp the edges together.
4. Use your fingers or a fork to crimp the edges of the top and bottom slices of bread together and form a "carriage," or pocket, around the mozzarella.
5. Pour about an inch or two of flour into a shallow pan or bowl; add salt and pepper to taste and mix it well with the flour.
6. Crack the two eggs into a bowl and beat until blended.
7. Add the flour to the half and half and stir well.
8. Dredge the mozzarella in carrozza in the eggs, then in the cream and flour mixture until coated.
9. Place about 2 inches of oil into a pan and heat on medium.

10. Carefully place the mozzarella in carrozza into the hot oil and cook on each side until golden brown, less than a minute per side. Only cook a few at a time, to avoid crowding the pan.
11. Remove the mozzarella in carrozza and place on a plate lined with paper towels.
12. Serve warm with a fresh marinara.

Osso Buco Milanese Style

This dish's name literally translates to bone (osso) with a hole (buco) because of the veal shank used in the recipe.

The dish is hearty and flavorful, great for cold weather, but not too heavy to eat any time of the year.

You can serve it with risotto Milanese (recipe given in this chapter).

Serving size: 4

Ingredients:

4 veal shanks, about 1½ inches thick

2 tablespoons of yellow onion

12 oz. can tomatoes

6 oz. white mushrooms, washed

2 carrots, peeled and thinly sliced

1 tablespoon parsley

1 cup chicken broth

1 cup white wine

1 tablespoon unsalted butter

1 oz. white flour

Extra-virgin olive oil

Salt and pepper to taste

Directions:

1. Dice the onions and parsley.
2. Chop the tomatoes into small pieces.
3. Rinse the mushrooms well and dry them, then thinly slice them.
4. Heat the olive oil in a skillet over medium heat.
5. Dredge each veal shank in the flour, then sear it in the pan on both sides until brown.
6. In a separate skillet, sauté the onions and thinly sliced carrots in butter until lightly golden.
7. Add the tomatoes and carrots to the onion and cook for five minutes.
8. Place the veal shank in the skillet with the vegetables, then add the wine and cook for five minutes.
9. Add the chicken broth and mushrooms. Cook for 5 to 7 minutes.
10. Add the butter and parsley, then salt and pepper the dish to taste.
11. Cook slowly at medium-low heat for 30 minutes, flipping the meat every few minutes.
12. Check that the veal reaches a temperature of 145 degrees and the meat is white throughout, to the bone.
13. Serve with risotto Milanese.

Gnocchi with Spinach

I love to make these dense potato dumplings with spinach to create a smooth texture and a light green shade.

These go well as a side dish to a protein entrée or as a main course, depending on the sauce you use.

Serving size: 4

Ingredients:

10 large russet potatoes

2 cups of fresh spinach

4 egg yolks

2 egg whites

1 teaspoon salt

½ teaspoon pepper

Flour in a quantity equal to the amount of the potatoes

Directions:

1. Peel the potatoes and dice them into uniform sized cubes; boil until they are thoroughly cooked and you can easily pierce a cube with a fork.
2. Drain the potatoes, then pass them through a vegetable strainer.
3. Boil the spinach until it starts to turn slightly mushy.
4. Drain the spinach and place it in a blender; puree it.
5. Combine the potatoes, spinach, flour, egg, salt, and pepper in a bowl (or form a mound on a cutting board with a hole in the middle for your wet ingredients). Mix well until a dough forms.
6. Take a handful of the mixture and roll it into a long tube about 1½ inches around.
7. Cut 1-inch pieces from the tube at an angle and press the tines of a fork onto the piece.
8. Repeat this until all the dough is used.
9. Boil water and cook the gnocchi for about 3 to 5 minutes; the gnocchi should rise to the top of the water when ready.
10. Drain and serve with your favorite sauce.

Lasagna Verde alla Bolognese

This lasagna includes spinach in the dough to give the pasta a green color.

Serving size: 10

Ingredients:

Bolognese meat sauce (see the sauce part of the Fettucine alla Bolognese recipe)

Bechamel sauce (see the following recipe on the following page)

10 cups semolina all-purpose flour

Buttermilk

Salt

Grated Parmigiano Reggiano cheese

8 egg yolks

2 eggs

1 cup of spinach puree

Salt and pepper to taste

Directions:

1. Mix the flour with the buttermilk, spinach, eggs, and egg yolks in a bowl or on a cutting board; mix until blended and smooth.
2. Pass the dough through a pasta machine.
3. Let the pasta dough set for two hours.
4. Cook the pasta in a large pot of boiling water for 2 to 3 minutes.
5. Prepare the Bolognese sauce and béchamel, then stir them together in a pan and heat.
6. Place sauce on the bottom of a 9 x 12 stainless steel pan.
7. Place a layer of pasta on the sauce. Continue alternating layers of sauce and pasta until you have four to five layers.
8. Cook for 8 to 10 minutes in a 350-degree oven.
9. Spread a layer of parmigiano cheese on the lasagna and heat in the oven for two minutes until the cheese melts and begins to brown.

Bechamel sauce

This sauce is a classic in French cuisine, and the basis for many types of other sauces.

Ingredients:

2 cups whole milk

1 cup flour

3 tablespoons butter

Directions:

1. Make a roux by melting the butter in a saucepan over medium heat, then slowly stirring in the flour until smooth.
2. Bring milk almost to a boil, then pour the milk slowly into the roux, stirring constantly.
3. Stir until combined.

Branzino alla Grillia

This dish uses a lovely fish called a branzino, or European bass. It has a meat close in flavor to red snapper.

Serving size: 2

Ingredients:

1 branzino (European bass), about 1½ lbs.

1 tablespoon minced garlic

½ cup Italian parsley

3 tablespoons extra-virgin olive oil

Juice of 1 lemon

Dash of cayenne pepper

Directions:

1. Finely chop the parsley and mince the garlic.
2. Clean the fish and remove the scales.
3. Make a marinade by combining the garlic, parsley, dash of cayenne, lemon juice, and olive oil in a bowl large enough to hold the fish.
4. Make a cut across both sides of the fish on each side of the midline between the head and tail. Place the fish in the marinade and let it marinate for at least two hours.
5. Place a cast iron grill on top of the stove and heat it to medium.
6. When the grill is hot, cook the fish for one minute on each side, starting to brown.
7. Place more marinade on it and finish cooking the fish in a 325-degree oven until the bones you can see through the cuts turn white.
8. Serve the fish with roast potatoes or your favorite side dish.

Roasted Rosemary Potatoes

This is a great, simple side dish for many types of proteins.

Serving size: 2

Ingredients:

1 cup diced russet potatoes

Dried rosemary

Extra-virgin olive oil

Salt and pepper to taste

Directions:

1. Spread the potatoes on a baking sheet.
2. Drizzle a little olive oil all over the potatoes.
3. Sprinkle the dried rosemary on the potatoes.
4. Add salt and pepper to taste.
5. Bake in a 325-degree oven until the potatoes start to turn brown and crispy.

Broccoli

This is my very simple broccoli recipe that the 41st President of the United States, George H. W. Bush, enjoyed. This was high praise from the President who famously proclaimed he didn't like broccoli.

Serving size: 4

Ingredients:

1 head of broccoli

Extra-virgin olive oil

1 clove of garlic

Salt and pepper to taste

Directions:

1. Slice the broccoli into small, even sized pieces; thinly slice the garlic clove.
2. Heat the olive oil in a pan over medium heat.
3. Sautee the broccoli until it starts to brown slightly.
4. Remove the broccoli from the pan and add a little olive oil to the pan.
5. Sautee the garlic in the oil until browned.
6. Toss the broccoli in the pan with the garlic.
7. Add salt and pepper to taste.

Fotografie: Photographs

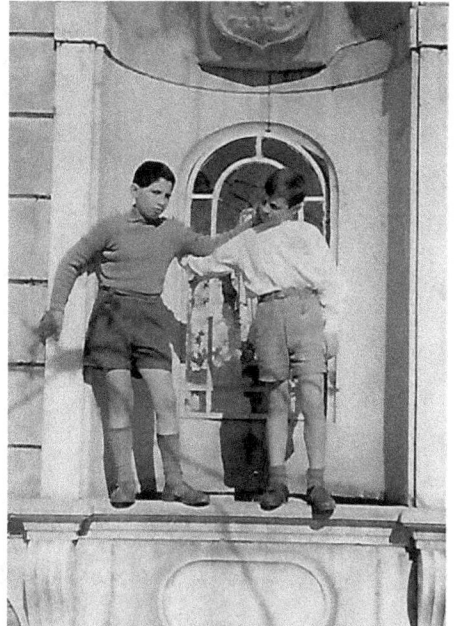

My friend Carlo and I taking a break from making mischief.

Me riding the yellow bike my mama bought me.

My sweet mama shortly before she passed away.

The letter verifying my first job in the restaurant business at The Caffe' Ristorante "Grand Italia" in Milano.

Me and a few feathered friends in Milan; I was fascinated with birds from a young age.

Me and my mates clowning around in England.

Here I am with a co-worker, dressed as pirates, for a huge party at the Princess hotel in Bermuda.

Posing by the amazing waters of Bermuda, where I learned to swim.

My bride Sofia and me on our wedding day.

The realization of my life-long dream: my own restaurant in Houston, Texas; it was located near the famous Galleria shopping area.

Open for business at my very own restaurant— not bad for someone with no formal education.

Showing off the patio of La Trattoria for al fresco dining.

The Texas Monthly write-up of my restaurant.

The restaurant's cleanliness award from the Houston TV personality, Marvin Zindler.

A proclamation honoring the restaurant's 26th anniversary by Rick Perry, Governor of the State of Texas.

My extensive wine cellar, deemed one of the best in the U.S. by the publication *Wine Spectator*.

The wine cellar, patterned after Brückenkeller's cellar, where I worked in Germany.

Me with the restaurant's menu and a bottle of Borgogno, a classic Italian wine.

Tyson and Maya enjoying spaghetti, much like the dogs from that famous Disney movie.

In my native element, the restaurant's kitchen; I only use the freshest ingredients in my dishes.

Me standing in front of my old school in Italy.

Me with my brothers standing in front of our old home.

My return visit to Milan, over 30 years after I left.

About the Author

Chef Carlo Molinaro is a self-taught chef with over 50 years of experience in the restaurant business. Carlo was born in Italy during World War II, pulled from school during an early age, and made to work.

He has worked in numerous countries around the world, working his way up from busboy to successful restaurant owner in Houston, TX.

He believes that if he can make it with only a 2nd grade education, anyone came succeed as well, by being disciplined and respectful. "Do your best, and money and success will follow," is one of Carlo's favorite sayings.

Although he sold his restaurant after 28 years, he still works occasionally as a chef in Houston. He has a daughter and granddaughter living in California.

John Dees has worked as a writer for over 30 years, contributing to newspapers, magazines, textbooks, technical publications, and videos. He lives in Central Texas with his family and his granddaughter Emma.

www.ingramcontent.com/pod-product-compliance
Lightning Source LLC
Chambersburg PA
CBHW051148290426
44108CB00019B/2650